Proactive Pastoral Counseling

Proactive Pastoral Counseling

An Intrapersonal Approach for Cultivating Christian Formation

Yaron I. Kohen

WIPF & STOCK · Eugene, Oregon

PROACTIVE PASTORAL COUNSELING
An Intrapersonal Approach for Cultivating Christian Formation

Copyright © 2025 Yaron I. Kohen. All rights reserved. Except for brief quotations in critical publications or reviews, no part of this book may be reproduced in any manner without prior written permission from the publisher. Write: Permissions, Wipf and Stock Publishers, 199 W. 8th Ave., Suite 3, Eugene, OR 97401.

Wipf & Stock
An Imprint of Wipf and Stock Publishers
199 W. 8th Ave., Suite 3
Eugene, OR 97401

www.wipfandstock.com

PAPERBACK ISBN: 979-8-3852-3102-7
HARDCOVER ISBN: 979-8-3852-3103-4
EBOOK ISBN: 979-8-3852-3104-1

VERSION NUMBER 06/23/25

All scriptures are taken from the THE HOLY BIBLE, NEW AMERICAN STANDARD BIBLE (NASB), Copyright© 1960, 1962, 1963, 1968, 1971, 1972, 1973, 1975, 1977, 1995 by The Lockman Foundation. Used by permission.

This book is dedicated to all those who have endured hardship in their walk with Christ due to the oppressive weight of religious legalism, the lure of radical individualism, the self-centeredness of sacro-egoism, the confusion of moral relativism, and the unrepentant hearts of those who bear the name of Jesus Christ in vain.

May this book serve as a reminder to all who seek the Lord that God reigns supreme, seated on His throne with unwavering love and justice that will never fail. Stand firm, Christian, for there is always hope in God through Jesus Christ. No matter how great the trials of life may be, always surrender to the power of the Holy Spirit to sustain and strengthen you.

Therefore, if God loves you so deeply that He gave His Son, Jesus, to die for your sins, and if the enemy seeks nothing less than to destroy your soul, know this: you are of infinite worth—more precious than eternity itself. So, remain rooted in the unshakable Rock of Christ, and you will dwell in the house of the Lord forever!

Contents

Preface | ix
Acknowledgments | xi
Abbreviations | xiii

1 The Fight for Spiritual Truth | 1
2 Nature, Tenets, and Applications of PPC | 28
3 How *Proactive* Pastoral Counseling Works | 58
4 The Efficacy of PPC Among Believers | 76
5 Conclusion | 111

Appendix A | 129
Appendix B: PPC Therapy Comparison List—
  Proactive *Pastoral Counseling* | 132
Appendix C: Proactive Pastoral Counseling
  Scriptural Foundations | 134
Bibliography | 157
Subject Index | 163
Scripture Index | 167

Preface

GOD SUPPLIES ALL GRACE and truth through our Savior, Jesus Christ, instilling His people with complete joy in knowing the supremacy of the Holy Spirit convicts and empowers change in the individual willing to receive grace.[1]

It is exhilarating to grasp that God's grace is freely available to all willing to embrace Jesus Christ as their Lord and Savior. Change is of the essence, but complete transformation is possible for those who allow the Holy Spirit to work in their lives, no matter their heart condition, past or present. However, despite many professing grace in the name of Christianity, many live as though they have not personally experienced the transformative power of the Holy Spirit.

Some might suggest their ability to discern spiritual matters has been inhibited by selfish desires, ambitions, and visions of self-centered grandeur. This observation is particularly noticeable among church leaders who, despite their spiritual roles, display spiritual blindness, leading to increased spiritual conflict within the fellowship of believers. If only those who claim to follow Christianity could recognize the pride within themselves. If the church redirected its selfish-centered focus from pursuing image, wealth, power, and control toward embodying Christlikeness in thought and behavior, its members, too, following the example of Christlikeness, might draw nearer to Christ themselves.

1. Stokes, "Heart, Soul, Mind, and Strength," 60.

Preface

Regardless of denomination, every Christian congregation should strive for godliness. The body of Christ exists to pursue Christlikeness and emulate the teachings of Jesus Christ, becoming more like God's Son through the power of the Holy Spirit. This spiritual purpose entails shifting from *secular to biblical* thinking, ensuring that every thought aligns with the obedience of Jesus Christ. Therefore, the church's declaration must continue to proclaim that there is hope for all who seek first His righteousness. Come to Christ. Be reconciled to God.

The church's mission is to believe in God's Word and follow Christ—to live according to God's will. One might ask, "Does today's Christian church gather on Sundays for its personal agendas or to worship God in Spirit and truth? Has today's church turned into a social club filled with 'doing' Christian events just for the sake of one saying, 'I am a Christian. I go to church and do Christian things like you'?" One might also ask, "Where is Christ?"

For the sake of future Christians, we must pray that today's church reprioritizes its motivations and community mindset, embracing Christian intrapersonal formation to safeguard its future members. Renewal will come to the church community if Christ becomes the central desire and motivation in believers' hearts and minds. The church must reexamine, relocate, and reenergize its goals and objectives—strive to resemble the world less and refocus on Christ on the cross as the center of its thinking. If the body of Christ fails in this pursuit, Christians will become nothing more than what Paul describes in 1 Corinthians 4:13b: "We have become as the scum of the world, the dregs of all things, even until now."

Acknowledgments

GOD IS A MIND-BLOWING *God!* Never in my life did I imagine writing a book about pastoral counseling. Who would have ever thought that I, Rev. Dr. Yaron I. Kohen, one day would contribute to its tenets and applications by implementing the Christian Integrative Therapeutic (CIT) called *Proactive* Pastoral Counseling (PPC), a new integrative approach for cultivating Christian Intrapersonal Formation (CIF)?

In retrospect, pastoral counseling was entirely unfamiliar to me throughout my churchgoing days as a youth—it was unavailable at my church or anywhere else. Interestingly, I was utterly oblivious to the world of pastoral counseling or its purpose until my church life as an adult began experiencing internal conflict. Besides, even if I had known about its tenets and applications then, I still would not have considered attending a pastoral counseling session—I was too rebellious. Besides, how can you recognize in yourself a need for spiritual encouragement when you cannot recognize spiritual things, let alone accept they exist?

In that light, I gratefully proclaim with the highest acknowledgment to my Lord: thank You, God, for completely blowing my mind and giving me the ability to discern spiritual things. Thank You for always pursuing me with Your love, guiding me toward a deeper understanding of my need for You. Thank You for filling me with the Holy Spirit, empowering me to wholly surrender in

Acknowledgments

humility to the power of Your Word, and submitting forever to Your will for my life!

I also would like to thank you, Dr. Dwight C. Rice, for your professional outlook as a reader of my doctoral thesis, from which the composition of this book originates. Likewise, your pastoral leadership has been a pivotal force in helping me become the Christian minister that I am today. Your immeasurable insights into pastoral counseling have refined and shaped me in more ways than you can imagine. Having such a captive audience with someone of your intellectual caliber and spiritual wisdom has been nothing less than an honor and a privilege—words cannot fully express my appreciation. Thank you for helping me find and reach my GPS!

Above all, I am deeply grateful to God for my doctoral mentor and friend, Dr. John S. Knox, whose unwavering guidance and editing prowess have made the writing of this book a true success. Dr. Knox, you are my "Ambassador of Quan," for without your knowledge, wisdom, and profound ability to guide me through the writing process, this book may never have become the blessing readers can now enjoy. I aspire to become as skilled a writer and teacher as you. Words cannot express my gratitude for helping me mature in these areas.

Thank you!

Abbreviations

CBT	*Cognitive Behavior Therapy*
CCT	*Christian Cognitive Therapy*
CE	*Christian Education*
CIF	*Christian Intrapersonal Formation*
CIT	*Christian Integrative Therapeutic*
IP	*Integrative Perspective*
IT	*Integrative Therapy*
NT	*Narrative Therapy*
PPC	*Proactive Pastoral Counseling*
REBT	*Rational Emotive Behavior Therapy*
SM	*Stephen Ministry / Stephen Minister*

— 1 —

The Fight for Spiritual Truth

THE QUEST FOR SPIRITUAL truth and discernment fills the hearts and minds of people across the globe.[1] While growing intrapersonally (i.e., the world inside a person's mind) in Christ has become a daily struggle for faithful Christians, many in church leadership, too, have suffered from the inability to manage their lives biblically. Today's average norm for many Christian congregations has become preference-driven gatherings devoted to self-preservation with personal agendas,[2] decreasing their capacity to know the truth and discern spiritual things. Unfortunately, the body of Christ has considerably digressed in its competence to manage intrapersonal conflict in themselves and others.

As a result, the aptitude of church leadership to spiritually lead its people has dramatically diminished. Church membership throughout most denominations has declined tremendously in recent years while simultaneously struggling to provide proper biblical leadership for the people. Unfortunately, the pursuit of being a Christ-centered church for each other and their communities has

1. Leaf, "Maintaining a Biblical Worldview," 108.
2. Fischer, *Albion's Seed*, 18.

caused significant suffering within the hearts and minds of those seeking spiritual rest.

What is causing the Christian to fall? Why is today's Christian church (the body of Christ) so unsuccessful in teaching biblical truths? One might suggest this ongoing issue stems from the lack of godly leadership within the church walls, highlighting the lack of competence of its spiritual leaders to educate others on how the Bible applies to the lives of everyday people. If this is the case, how can Christians and gospel-centered churches become the people God designed them to become? The answer: pursue Christian intrapersonal formation.

Christian Intrapersonal Formation (CIF)

Christian intrapersonal formation happens when Christlikeness becomes one's mental focal point. In other words, cognitive formation in Christ occurs when biblical thinking supersedes self-centered thinking in all areas of one's life. The shift from secular to biblical thinking transforms the believer's intrapersonal world and generates new thoughts that lead to new behaviors—behaviors that God approves. But how can one experience Christian intrapersonal formation?

Proactive Pastoral Counseling (PPC)

Proactive Pastoral Counseling (PPC) is a Christian Integrative Therapeutic (CIT) approach designed to foster Christian intrapersonal formation in believers. Guided by a *proactive* pastoral counselor, the Christian Intrapersonal Formation (CIF) training program—a structured four-step process—encourages individuals to engage with God's Word deeply and with deliberate intentions for changing internally. In so doing, the interactive nature of the CIF program aims to lead individuals away from self-centered thinking and toward Christlike behavior by applying biblical principles to everyday thoughts and actions. Spiritual growth occurs as one consciously strives for a mindset toward Christlikeness. But how can one recognize progress in their journey of intrapersonal growth in Christ?

Many agree that spiritual formation is an inner transformation facilitated by the grace of God. Essentially, "Spiritual formation is the manifestation of God's grace in the hearts and actions of individuals."[3] In this context, the CIF four-step training program encourages individuals to engage in "self-reflection in Christ," aiding them in confronting and overcoming self-centered thinking. The CIF process guides people to reassess and reshape their life stories through the perspective of God's grace and His Word.

By embracing Christian spiritual disciplines, such as meditating on God's Word, individuals enhance their capacity to grasp divine truths. Understanding how to apply God's Word helps people discern spiritual matters more deeply. Many who have undergone Christian intrapersonal formation frequently express, "There is no greater journey in life than exploring the mind to cultivate Christlike thinking."

Simultaneously, the shift from self-centered to biblical thinking profoundly impacts the spiritual health of believers. The Bible teaches that those who repent and accept Jesus Christ as their Savior experience a transformative renewal through the Holy Spirit's work of regeneration, resulting in a new nature. This inner transformation empowers individuals to adopt a worldview aligned with the mindset of Christ.[4] Christian intrapersonal formation training helps others detect and deter non-Christian thought patterns, fostering an attitude rooted in Christian principles and diminishing intrapersonal conflicts.

While the pursuit of many Christian denominations seeks to grow intrapersonally in Christ, churches maintain their struggle to provide an appropriate pastoral counseling approach that can penetrate the self-centered consciousness that dominates the minds of believers today. In that light, PPC and the CIF approach accomplish that goal by focusing on biblically inspired spiritual

---

3. Maddix, "Spiritual Formation," 12.
4. Leaf, "Maintaining a Biblical Worldview," 7.

applications in a group setting facilitated by a *proactive* pastoral counselor.[5]

Summary

Proactive Pastoral Counseling (PPC) is a new integrative approach to addressing Christian intrapersonal formation in believers. PPC, co-laboring with Christian Intrapersonal Formation (CIF), a four-step *proactive* pastoral counseling program, targets intrapersonal conflict that disrupts the hearts and minds of God-fearing men and women from living out God's plan for their lives. For example, instead of looking only at the problem, PPC asks, "Why is the problem a problem to you? What is causing you to experience intrapersonal conflict?" In essence, PPC and the CIF program help people see their lives from a biblical perspective, drawing them away from self-centered thinking while assisting them to reframe intrapersonal conflict with the power of God's wisdom.

Church of Sardis (Church S)

Too many churches in America today are experiencing an increased need for Christian intrapersonal formation. For comparison, one might consider Jesus' words about the church of Sardis in Revelation 3:1–4 as a reminder for today's Christians about the importance of seeking God's Word for spiritual truth and understanding (John 6:63). Suppose today's church and church leaders continue to preach God's Word without the leading of the Holy Spirit and refrain from teaching others how to submit to His voice. In that case, the present Christian church will digress and continue diminishing.

In that respect, the following represents anecdotes based on the life of an authentic church in a real community with real people dealing with real struggles. However, the names and places

---

5. Wells and Dickens, "Creativity in Counselor Education," 197.

have been omitted or changed to protect their privacy. For all intents and purposes, *Church S* will represent this cause.

Church S

Church S is a small conservative body of Christ nestled in the pristine woods of New England's countryside. Its membership ranges between twenty and forty active and inactive members yearly. Some adolescents attend randomly, but it is mostly home to parishioners aged sixty to eighty-five. Its constitution and bylaws govern its members and operate as an autonomous church body.

Church S offers traditional (9:30 a.m.) and contemporary (11 a.m.) worship services. The standard service preserves the older church worship style and devotes its structure toward a conventional liturgy, such as a call to worship, reading of Old Testament and New Testament Scriptures, receiving the offering, a pastoral prayer, an expository sermon, and enjoying songs from the traditional Baptist hymnal accompanied by a piano player. The contemporary service provides a spirited worship team that leads the congregation with a modern style of Christ-centered music using acoustic and bass guitars, piano, and inspired vocals. Comparatively, both the traditional and contemporary services employ a Christian pastor who preaches God's Word from a transparent, dynamic, gospel-centered heart and encourages others to renew their hearts and minds in the Spirit of Christ.[6]

Additionally, the weekly ministry of *Church S* includes Sunday School with the pastor on Sunday nights, Wednesday night prayer meetings, a men's and women's breakfast taking place every second and fourth Saturday morning, weekly Bible studies (individual and group settings for teaching spiritual truths to promote Christian intrapersonal growth),[7] and once a month seniors gather for food, fun, fellowship, and games.

---

6. The sermons of the writer of this book can be found at https://www.Youtube.com/@GraceMinistriesforChrist.

7. Morley, *Man's Guide*, 42.

Every quarter, on the first Sunday of the month, *Church S* conducts a worship service centered on the Lord's Supper. The church's doctrine emphasizes the deity and person of the crucified Christ Jesus, His resurrection, and His eventual return to gather His followers; salvation comes solely through faith in the name of Christ Jesus. Baptisms occur in swimming pools during the winter when facilities are available, and in the summer, they typically happen in the nearest pond or lake.

In addition to baptisms, *Church S*'s member board, which comprises folks from various backgrounds and walks of life, makes decisions concerning church membership, property use, and finances. On the last Sunday of each month, the members of *Church S* gather to discuss the daily operations, review the treasurer's report, discuss old business, and introduce any new business pertinent to growing the ministry at *Church S*. Occasionally, weddings, benefit dinners, celebrations of life, and special music events help encourage new life among its parishioners *and* the community.

The congregation at *Church S* predominantly comprises an older generation who have lived rich and varied lives. Among them are former minor league baseball players, collegiate athletes, coaches, professional cribbage players, fish and game wardens, schoolteachers, photographers, artists, shoemakers, foresters, business owners, and stay-at-home moms. These individuals carry forward the legacy of the "old heroes" from their past. Generally, they are traditional, hardworking people who have led fulfilling lives and now enjoy the comforts of retirement.

Demographic

The members of *Church S* cherished the sense of community they built together over the years, finding gratification, self-worth, and accomplishment in their hard work. However, amidst their daily lives, they lost sight of God's will for them and their purpose in the community, resisting the guidance of the Holy Spirit. Historically, the witness of the Spirit and the concept of perfect love, as taught by Wesley, were dismissed as a harmful delusion.[8] Eventually, religious legalism replaced the experience of God's grace at *Church S*. Regrettably, following the Holy Spirit became a rigid and uninspired objective for both the church and its community members. Consequently, the congregation of *Church S* gradually succumbed to spiritual apathy and inaction, finding solace in the rigid confines of religious legalism as their guiding principle for personal conduct and judgment of others. Over time, *Church S* erected invisible barriers, effectively isolating itself from long-standing and emerging demographics in the surrounding area, unwilling to adhere to its stringent norms. Thus, despite demographic shifts unfolding in the community over the years, the internal dynamics of the church in New England have stagnated.[9] This disconnect ushered *Church S* into a downward spiral of spiritual decline. However, one must ask, "What caused the spiritual descent at *Church S*?"

Realistically, many *Church S* members resisted the Holy Spirit's transformative work. As a result, church membership dwindled, and nonmembers drifted away. The church's spiritual leaders, who operated with a narrow, religious mindset, limited any proposed efforts toward community outreach, leading to a spiritual decline within the church.[10] Over time, *Church S* developed a reputation for being nothing other than judgmental, self-centered, and focused on personal preferences rather than reflecting a grace-filled body of Christ dedicated to reaching out to the broken and lost.

Much like the men Paul references in Acts 7:51, *Church S* was obstinate and spiritually unresponsive, consistently resisting the guidance of the Holy Spirit. The community saw that *Church S* adhered rigidly to religious mandates, where the grace of Christ was nothing more than a line in a book.[11] The members relied on self-understanding to manage their church life and behavior rather than embracing one another in God's truth and pursuing authentic

---

8. Pilsbury and Allen, *History of Methodism*, 4.
9. Rhodes, "Discipling Leadership," 6.
10. Millet, *History of the Baptists*, 213.
11. Rainer, *Autopsy of a Deceased Church*, 25–30.

Christian spirituality.¹² In essence, the hearts and minds of the believers at *Church S* rejected any form of Christian spiritual formation, leading to irrevocable suffering for the entire community.¹³

Suffering from spiritual disengagement, *Church S* lost sight of its purpose for itself and the community. It became spiritually blinded, leading to a breakdown in godly relationships between the church and the broader community. A spirit of intolerance took root, deceitful behavior toward its members increased, and gossip replaced honest storytelling. Fear of open communication grew, religious implications were exaggerated, and the concept of living by the Spirit became a distant and neglected ideal.¹⁴ Today, *Church S* continues to impose a judgmental religious attitude on others and suffers greatly from not striving toward Christlikeness. Still, there is more to consider.

New England tradition suggests that deeply ingrained "Puritan" influences controlled the hearts and minds of its inhabitants.¹⁵ For instance, religious requirements imposed by their ancestors mandated that *Church S* maintain a spirit of religiosity. This inherited focus on upholding religious mandates enabled each generation to continue enforcing standards of judgmentalism and exclusivity based solely on self-derived interpretations from the past.¹⁶ Subsequently, instead of attending church to worship the Lord sincerely, parishioners began to gather out of fear of judgment from their peers, perpetuating the internal conflicts established by their forbearers.¹⁷ This religious opposition ultimately became the force that kept the Spirit of Christ away from the hearts and minds of the people at *Church S*.¹⁸

In view, gatherings at *Church S* eventually became nothing more than a social event and a way to hold others accountable to

---

12. Millet, *History of the Baptists*, 213.
13. Millet, *History of the Baptists*, 213.
14. Millet, *History of the Baptists*, 213.
15. Pilsbury and Allen, *History of Methodism*, 6.
16. Pilsbury and Allen, *History of Methodism*, 6.
17. Millet, *History of the Baptists*, 23.
18. Pilsbury and Allen, *History of Methodism*, 6.

its religious mandates. Essentially, *Church S* sought the approval of others instead of pursuing Christlikeness, creating a false sense of character in people. As Paul describes in 1 Timothy 4:1–2, the spirit of deceit ruled the hearts and minds of the people through the hypocrisy of liars. The "pretend" nature of *Church S* created a false sense of Christianity and Christian conduct in its members, and they became frightened of being honest with others for fear of being found out and shunned (for various offenses).[19]

Furthermore, the church fostered duplicitous behavior, and those in the community experienced a deep-rooted separation from churchgoing townsfolk. The separation between the church and community became so distinct that church membership declined from sixty-two in earlier years to nineteen members.[20] According to the testimonies of many long-term residents, the main reason for the disconnect between the church and the community stems from an elitist, judgmental presence and attitude that *Church S* imposes on those in the community.[21] Incidentally, people at *Church S* became so untrustworthy that they employed spiritual oppression as a means of controlling the people inside the church walls.

More so, religious legalism and judgment became *Church S*'s primary vehicle to manipulate established members and new members into retaining their membership, and there is some evidence for this. Like the Pharisees accused Jesus (Jesus committed no crime), *Church S* also treated others in the exact likeness by instituting the custom of judging one another before hearing the

19. Eubanks, *How We Relate*, 231.

20. The church record that provides this information has been withheld in order to protect the identity of *Church S*.

21. The author interviewed many long-term residents to learn about the stories about *Church S* that have been passed down through the generations. Six months of field research was compiled together to create an accurate assessment. Multiple stories were told as to why people do not attend *Church S*. However, out of all the personal one-on-one interviews given (over a hundred), the most common reason folks in town do not attend *Church S* stems from its religious, legalistic, and judgmental behavior towards others. In contrast, they cannot see themselves from this perspective—spiritually undiscerning and absent from knowing biblical truths.

truth (John 7:51)—*Church S* chose what to believe about people regardless of any truth. Irrational behavior established the norm at *Church S*, dictating how members and nonmembers experience religious gatherings, which partially explains why the same behavior persists at *Church S* today.

Like their forefathers, *Church S* behaved falsely toward themselves, others, and God, personifying in themselves what "pretend" Christians look like, as noted in Matthew 15:8–9. Similarly, as Paul notes in 1 Thessalonians 2:4, proper Christian behavior comes from the desire to become approved by God. In contrast, *Church S* still does not "imitate" the likeness of Paul (1 Cor 11:1), nor do they seek the approval of God's will and direction for the life of their church body.

Considering this perspective, if the apostle Paul were to visit *Church S* and fail to conform to their specific practices, he would face severe judgment for not adhering to their religious mandates. He would inevitably be shunned and become an outcast. As previously highlighted, this same issue continues to permeate the congregation of *Church S* today. Membership remains stagnant, and the generationally induced spiritual disconnect prevents the church and community from living harmoniously. Without godly leadership or reforms to proactively prepare the hearts and minds of this body of Christ, the parishioners of *Church S* risk losing the battle for Christian spiritual formation and may ultimately be forced to close their doors permanently.[22]

The Problem of *Church S*

For years, *Church S* lacked "shepherd" leadership to equip its congregants with the spiritual tools necessary for Christian intrapersonal formation. Although various speakers occasionally took the pulpit, non-spiritual leaders of *Church S*—often referred to as the control group—heavily influenced the thoughts and spiritual direction of those they trained as lay leaders or pursued as full-time

---

22. Macchia, *Discerning Life*, 88.

THE FIGHT FOR SPIRITUAL TRUTH

pastors. Similarly, *Church S*'s control group imposed their own religious rules on how established members and new members should live a Christian life rather than be an example of Christian living. They failed to provide the presence of a Christlike attitude, as Paul described in Philippians 2:1–5, which created a sense of religious stoicism and lack of heartfelt joy for others.

In other words, *Church S* suffered from a mass consciousness of strict religious legalism and judgment, sternly holding one another accountable for their behavioral failures. Intense internal spiritual damage persisted, relationships split apart, and people's hearts turned against one another, creating an environment of intrapersonal conflict with no one to lead them out. Holding to religious-minded leadership, one might suggest a misaligned outlook between doctrine and ministry suppressed the Spirit within the church (1 Thess 5:19).

Nonetheless, the control group of *Church S* generated significant interpersonal chaos within its church walls. Members and nonmembers suffered from low self-esteem due to the fear of rejection or the prospect of being publicly shunned. Many lost the confidence needed to pursue God through Christ, as Paul describes in 2 Corinthians 3:4–6. Tragically, most failed to see themselves and others from a spiritually discerning perspective because the ability to discern spiritual truths was absent. In short, there was no repentance, causing spiritual decay.

Theologians commonly recall the condition and state of man, in that the natural man does not accept or understand the things of the Spirit, as Paul explains in 1 Corinthians 2:14. For example, A. W. Tozer, an esteemed pastor and theologian of nineteenth-century America, notes, "It is my observation that the natural man does not understand spiritual principles. The problem has never been the translation. The problem has never been academic. The problem has always been spiritual."[23] In that likeness, believers at *Church S* misunderstood doctrinal truths and spiritual insights

---

23. Tozer, *Crucified Life*, 19.

(even from its conception), hindering the church's moral beliefs, procedures, and teachings.[24]

In a parallel vein, the shortcomings of *Church S* in its spiritual outreach to the community left an unspoken but palpable shadow over perceptions of Christian doctrine and the essence of Christ's teachings. Wesley once grappled with the challenge, remarking, "Human language falls short in articulating divine truths."[25] Recollections from individuals rooted in the town's history passed down through generations via oral tradition underscore this sentiment: parents led their children to believe they lacked the capacity or knowledge to engage with the Bible, independently. In short, parents deemed it solely the clergy's prerogative to decipher its meaning. Thus, attending Sunday service became synonymous with passive reception, with the pastor serving as the sole conduit of understanding.[26]

Accordingly, a pervasive misapprehension of spiritual matters took root—the misunderstanding of spiritual things permeated. *Church S*'s failure to discern things spiritually and understand God's truth produced significant conflict between *Church S* and the community. Today, the spirit of deceit generated long ago between the church and the community continues, and intrapersonal conflict in its people dominates the religious scene. The problem is that *Church S* lacks intrapersonal spiritual health, resulting in interpersonal conflict and behavior that is unbecoming Christlikeness. Therefore, to address this problem, one must employ the tenets and applications of PPC.

---

24. Rhodes, "Discipling Leadership," 55.

25. Wesley, *Witness of the Spirit*, 3.

26. In a conversation on Oct. 15, Mr. Jones, who is in his mid-seventies, shared stories passed down from his parents and his personal experience growing up in town. One thing he remembers about his family church life is how he was not allowed to read the Bible because he was not able to understand it nor interpret what it said. Essentially, many congregants went to church just to hear what was in the Bible because many of them did not have Bibles nor were even allowed to open them. Some folks even did not know how to read.

Proactive Pastoral Counseling (PPC) Defined

The purpose of PPC is to equip and encourage believers to grow intrapersonally in Christ. Christian intrapersonal formation is the key to understanding God's truth, which manifests spiritual well-being.[27] Those who grasp the truth of God's Word can also discern whether change is personal gain or the type of gain Christ desires.[28] In other words, Christian intrapersonal formation might best describe itself as the result of practicing the preference for seeing God in everything.[29]

Christian Maturity

Furthermore, intentionally seeking God's guidance in everything enhances one's ability to discern spiritual matters. Applying the spiritual disciplines outlined in the Bible fosters this discernment and promotes more significant spiritual growth and maturity. For this growth to occur, spiritual leaders who have matured in the Spirit must implement biblical applications and guide others toward spiritual truths and discernment. In that sense, PPC becomes crucial for facilitating the Christian intrapersonal process.[30]

Christian maturity develops when life priorities change intentionally and shift from self-worship to worship of God.[31] In other words, living a discerning life is an intentional choice of the will.[32] Growing in Christ encompasses moving down the discipleship road and believing in doctrinal positions, but it also incorporates transforming into a specific type of person.[33] To become that person, one must seek out, practice, and employ spiritual disciplines, as well as learn how spending time in Christlikeness yields

27. Dodson, "Assessing Well-Being," 33.
28. Rhodes, "Discipling Leadership," 88–89.
29. Macchia, *Discerning Life*, 22.
30. Macchia, *Discerning Life*, 92.
31. Rhodes, "Discipling Leadership," 12.
32. Macchia, *Discerning Life*, 53.
33. Cheng et al., "Development and Validation," 69.

new character.³⁴ Christian intrapersonal formation is a Christlike means to make that happen—to create and inspire change in one's thought process.

Like spiritual and Christian formation, Christian intrapersonal formation involves a lifetime of transformation, a sanctification process providing salvation through Christ, as Paul addresses in Philippians 2:12–13. Through the gracious movement of God's Spirit, Christian intrapersonal formation allows others to hope for an abundant life in Christ for God's kingdom and glory and the fulfillment of his mission of grace, justice, mercy, and peace for all.³⁵ Ultimately, Christian intrapersonal formation, adult development, Christian formation, and spiritual formation measured in any believer is reflective of the life that one displays daily.³⁶

Basic Assumptions

Christian intrapersonal formation happens when biblical thinking precedes secular thinking, allowing the Holy Spirit to fill the mind. This cognitive process involves living purposefully in the presence of the Lord Jesus Christ, allowing God's Word to influence all thoughts and actions.³⁷ White explains, "While acknowledging that we make space for specific practices, it is critical to recognize that the work is God's. As we work out our salvation, 'God at work in [us]' accomplishes any real change or transformation. We cannot transform ourselves."³⁸ As Paul notes in 2 Corinthians 10:5, Christian intrapersonal formation occurs when one willingly accepts the Holy Spirit as the agent of cognitive change and daily takes his thoughts captive to the obedience of Christ.

Indeed, spiritual discipline, Christian spirituality, intrapersonal conflict, and pastoral counseling are areas that go beyond the

---

34. Harris, "Christocentric Discipleship," 17.
35. Macchia, *Discerning Life*, 22.
36. Marshall and Newheiser, *When Words Matter*, 91.
37. Marshall and Newheiser, *When Words Matter*, 40.
38. White, "Conceptualizing Therapy," 92.

current capacities or focus of *Church S*. Nevertheless, it is imperative to address these needs for the benefit of future parishioners. The hypothesis "To change a culture is to change the way it thinks" (i.e., change the words one uses to process thought) emphasizes biblical thinking over self-centered thinking to foster Christian intrapersonal formation among believers.

In the same spirit, it is crucial to remember that "the Christian Scriptures serve as the primary source for Christian spirituality. Our personal spiritual development is not based on a haphazard collection of favorite texts combined with individual circumstances. Instead, the Holy Spirit shapes us by following the teachings of the Holy Scriptures."[39]

For individual change to occur, though, something must change in its present setting;[40] when nothing changes, nothing changes, and cognitive health becomes limited. For this reason, a pastoral counselor must become *proactive* rather than reactive and offer additional resources and opportunities for spiritual growth and change.[41] Under submission to the Holy Spirit, the pastoral counselor intentionally guides an individual's thought process with God's Word so that His Word will work out and affect the intrapersonal world of those participating, resulting in Christian intrapersonal growth.[42]

At the same time, the Holy Spirit does not restrict Himself to boundaries made by men. As described in Acts 17:24, God does not dwell in temples made with hands, nor is He served by human hands as though He needed anything. In John 3:8, John preaches there is no way to measure, grant, limit, induce, control, impose, hinder (or the likeness of such things), or dictate the workings of God and the power of the Holy Spirit in anyone.[43] Moses proclaimed that God alone pours out His mercy on anyone, at any time, affecting change according to His will for a person's life

39. Haykin, *God Who Draws Near*, 63.
40. Van der Watt, "Mission-Minded Pastoral Theology," 7.
41. Dodson, "Assessing Well-Being," 147.
42. Stokes, "Heart, Soul, Mind, and Strength," 213.
43. White, "Conceptualizing Therapy," 93.

(Exod 33:19)—acknowledging that by the power of God alone can one's spiritual and intrapersonal world become affected.[44]

Ultimately, PPC and the CIF training program encourage all people who desire Christian intrapersonal development to come to Christ. No matter the shame, regret, feelings of unworthiness, or the number of times a person falls away from repentance, salvation comes through believing in the heart and confessing with the tongue that Jesus Christ is Lord (Rom 10:9–10). Therefore, Christian intrapersonal formation will occur in believers when the church allows the power of Christ instead of himself to invade the inner world of its people.

Definitions

This book uses standard and more complex terms and concepts to enhance one's understanding of a pastoral counseling approach that promotes Christian intrapersonal growth. Conceptual meaning and terminology include but are not limited to Christian education, Christian spirituality, intrapersonal conflict, intrapersonal formation, pastoral counseling, religious legalism, and "spirit of the mind" to provide more profound clarity. Introducing these specialized terms and concepts helps readers grasp the content more thoroughly, even if they are not part of a person's everyday language.

Christian Education

Christian Education (CE) advocates spirituality through training in Christlikeness, submitting to the authority of God's written word, established in Christ for His creation.[45] God provided grace and truth through the person and works of Jesus Christ (His life as a human being), through which His sacrifice on the cross (Christ in His flesh bore our sins), His resurrection (God raised Christ from the dead), and the return for His bride might draw men unto

---
44. Rhodes, "Discipling Leadership," 12.
45. Harris, "Christocentric Discipleship," 61.

Himself through the ministry and "word of reconciliation" (2 Cor 5:19). In essence, belief in the teachings of Christ founded on these principles and precepts gives CE its name and directs its approach in educating others from a Christian worldview perspective.[46]

Additionally, CE teaches the Christian worldview by promoting the creation of man, the fall, and human redemption as a part of God's plan for restoring sinners and becoming a new creation in Christ. Hessert notes, "Full education requires an understanding of the religious factor."[47] A worldview, then, is a conceptual lens through which we see, understand, and interpret the world and our place within it.[48] Overall, the impetus of this book maintains that God created all things and "upholds all things by the word of His power," which is in Christ (Heb 1:3).

With that in mind, CE also teaches righteousness as a faithful, genuine, and humble relationship with Christ, daily submitting oneself to God's commands, surrendering every thought captive to the obedience of Christ with a repentant heart while pursuing the likeness of Christ. Christian Education seeks to inform others about the purpose of godliness, holding steadfast in selflessness to gain favor with God and others.[49] Mckinney suggests a more nuanced understanding: for him, CE is "an educational process that produces Christians. CE seeks to develop its learners a strong belief in, dedication to, and knowledge of Jesus Christ so they can better know him, reflect his image in the world, and bring others to him."[50]

Nonetheless, for Christian intrapersonal formation to become realized, CE must inspire the process of growing the inner man—the heart, the spirit of the mind—by helping others disengage from their current intrapersonal world and reengage in Christlike thinking, such as in Bible reading and study, prayer, silence, and discipleship training measures. Whitney explains, "God's word is exclusive to spiritual discipline . . . godliness is its

46. Cheng et al., "Development and Validation," 67–68.
47. Hessert, *Introduction to Christianity*, 83.
48. Anderson et al., *Introduction to Christian Worldview*, 8.
49. Rice, "Story Tuning."
50. McKinney, *Christian Education*, 4.

only goal."[51] Hessert asserts, "When Christian education ceases to work, spiritual blindness increases."[52]

Consequently, by willfully adhering to the practices and principles found in Scripture and seeking out regeneration by the Holy Spirit, one becomes renewed in Christian development with a proper *telos* of conformity to the image of Christ.[53] Hence, CE emphasizes God's love for His creation, promoting hope through His promises. In other words, God supplies all the grace and knowledge of the Lord and Savior Jesus Christ, instilling His people with complete joy in knowing that the Holy Spirit convicts and empowers change in the individual willing to receive grace.[54]

Christian Intrapersonal Formation

Christian Intrapersonal Formation (CIF) promotes Christlikeness in a person's mind, heart, and spirit, resulting from intentional learning. Whitney affirms, "To follow Christ and become more like Him, we must engage in the Spiritual Discipline of learning."[55] Therefore, intrapersonal formation seeks empowerment from the Holy Spirit while submitting to biblical insights and applications for a transformed life. Herein lies the impetus behind PPC: to help others experience Christian intrapersonal formation.

One approach CIF utilizes is its ability to intentionally help others engage in self reflection in Christ through self-talk and interpersonal communication—providing a Christian safe space.[56] Christian safe spaces provide a nonjudgmental atmosphere to observe intrapersonal growth as participants solidify stronger relationships with others, particularly those providing

---

51. Whitney, *Spiritual Disciplines*, 4.
52. Hessert, *Introduction to Christianity*, 148.
53. Setran and Wilhoit, "Christian Education," 542.
54. Stokes, "Heart, Soul, Mind, and Strength," 60.
55. Whitney, *Spiritual Disciplines*, 273.
56. White, "Conceptualizing Therapy," 92.

pastoral counseling.⁵⁷ Self-reflection involves assessing one's inner world, such as how one thinks, feels, and manages intrapersonal factors.⁵⁸ Essentially, self-reflection in Christ is the key to healthy self-awareness.⁵⁹

Oleś mentions, "Internal dialogical activity shares a good deal of variance with common self-talk functions. In other words, there is a significant self-talk component to internal dialogues."⁶⁰ Yet, by applying the Christian worldview lens, an individual might learn how to self-reflect "in Christ," gaining biblical perspectives on any cognitive behavior that might create negative or irrational thinking about oneself or others.⁶¹ When relocation from self to Christ occurs, one's internal world changes and intrapersonal formation occurs.⁶²

Christian Spirituality

There is much debate on understanding the nature of spirituality, let alone attempting to define Christian spirituality from a natural premise. However, McClendon recommends, "As it relates to the development of Christian spirituality, the most significant meaning of Spirit is the indwelling presence of God's Spirit and the life that flows from that presence."⁶³ Macchia says, "Releasing the fullness of our attachments is profitable for the soul. A healthy dependence on God's Spirit to define and refine you as an individual and a group will lead you into a release posture. Letting go is what defines most of our spirituality and our maturity."⁶⁴

Stokes refers to the state of a deep relationship with God. He comments, "Christian spirituality is the outworking . . . of God's

57. Wells and Dickens, "Creativity in Counselor Education," 197.
58. White, "Conceptualizing Therapy," 92.
59. Vanderstelt et al., "Transformational Education," 94.
60. Oleś et al., "Types of Inner Dialogues," 9.
61. Liu et al., "Counselor Trainees' Personal Growth," 15.
62. Rhodes, "Discipling Leadership," 12.
63. McClendon, *Paul's Spirituality*, 1.
64. Macchia, *Discerning Life*, 155.

grace in the human soul, beginning with conversion and concluding with death or Christ's second advent. It is marked by growth and maturity in Christlike life."[65] Van der Watt explains, "Through the Holy Spirit, God's power is the power to create new life, to cure, and to rebuild rather than the power to impose, that is, to control."[66]

Ultimately, Christian spirituality is impossible to grasp without the indwelling of God's Spirit, which onto man He imputed from Himself after overcoming sin and death, to work in the inner man to become holy. Stokes adds, "Christian spirituality is the outworking of God's grace in the human soul beginning with conversion and concluding with death or Christ's second advent. It is marked by growth and maturity in Christlike life."[67] Therefore, the pursuit of godliness through Christ becomes realized as a process that undergoes a lifetime of spiritual training.[68]

Intrapersonal Conflict

Intrapersonal refers to the internal space (cognition) in which a person conducts, deals with, copes, and facilitates rational and irrational thinking. The intrapersonal world exists to process the inner workings of one's cognition, including any disruption that might affect the normal state of mental peace and overall spiritual well-being—those things that occur within oneself, particularly the mind. In a study of sixty-nine articles on peer assessment, Xiuyan identified six intrapersonal factors: motivation, self-efficacy, emotions, trust in the self as an assessor, fairness, and comfort.[69]

One might understand internal disruptions as the presence of cognitive dissonance that reveals the "self-talk" within oneself, exposing the inner workings that created the turmoil in the first

---

65. Stokes, "Heart, Soul, Mind, and Strength," 27.
66. Van der Watt, "Mission-Minded Pastoral Theology," 7.
67. Stokes, "Heart, Soul, Mind, and Strength," 27.
68. Whitney, *Spiritual Disciplines*, 6.
69. Guo et al., "Development and Validation," 1243.

place (such as spiritual integrity). Oleś explains, "When I have a difficult choice, I talk the decision over with myself from different points of view, and in my thoughts, I take the perspective of someone else. Such dialogues might involve taking a fruitful or conflicted perspective of another person."[70] In essence, intrapersonal conflict is nothing more than spiritually induced mental chaos in its pursuit of finding cognitive resolve.

However, within the parameters of Christian intrapersonal growth, intrapersonal resolve varies, depending on whether submission to godly thinking precedes worldly thinking in the individual. The resolution for intrapersonal conflict occurs when the thought process relocates from carnal disruption to a location that embodies Christian spirituality, such as replacing disruptive thoughts with thinking inspired by Scripture. The hope is to relocate one's internal infrastructure that produces thought without cognitive damage to the area of the desired change by finding mental and spiritual resolve through God's Word in Christ.

Intrapersonal vs. Spiritual

Throughout this book, the terms "spiritual" and "intrapersonal" might occasionally become interchangeable concerning meaning. The word "spiritual" generally suggests having a specific awareness of one's internal being from a natural sagacity; a spirit lives inside man, allowing him to move in the flesh.[71] "Intrapersonal" is the understanding from which one's feelings and thoughts become internally processed. Combined, both spiritual and intrapersonal can take on the same meaning in that to grow intrapersonally, one must also develop spiritually in nature.[72]

Holding to that premise, God's Word is the power that gives both spirit and life (John 6:63). As Paul describes in 1 Corinthians 2:11–14, God's Word, empowered by the Holy Spirit, is the only

---

70. Oleś et al., "Types of Inner Dialogues," 5.
71. Murray, *Humility*, 27.
72. Liu et al., "Counselor Trainees' Personal Growth," 24.

power that can open the hearts and minds of individuals to understand and discern spiritual things. Therefore, only by consuming God's Word and surrendering to the Holy Spirit can one process and understand inwardly the spiritual things of God.

Pastoral Counseling (Proactive)

The Christian worldview is the foundation for effective pastoral counseling, which helps individuals understand and cope with spiritual struggles that arise involuntarily. By integrating biblical applications, pastoral counseling addresses the spiritual needs of those in immediate crisis, known as reactive pastoral counseling.[73] Therefore, PPC recognizes pastoral counseling as its primary function but does so using a *proactive* approach. Instead of waiting for individuals to seek help, PPC forms small groups to intentionally target intrapersonal conflict before a person's mind becomes disenchanted from acknowledging the need for biblical guidance. Essentially, PPC brings pastoral counseling to clients outside the traditional office setting and beyond the church walls. Moreover, PPC employs a pastoral counselor as a CIT to build caring, trustworthy relationships with others.

Having that opportunity with others, PPC focuses on helping others experience CIF by intentionally targeting the cognitive struggle in others. As Wilkins states, "Christian counseling, in its purest form, is a covenant between a caregiver and a care seeker to labor collaboratively for the possession of the soul—through the power of the Holy Spirit, under the authority of the Word of God, and within a context of accountability and encouragement—for the purpose of the imitation of the Christ."[74] He adds, "Counseling from a Christian perspective covers a variety of problems for people: helping people deal with severe loss, conflict resolution,

---

73. Wilkins, "Educating the Congregation," 51.
74. Wilkins, "Educating the Congregation," 51.

stress management or elimination, and other issues that plague individuals."[75]

Pastoral counseling must consider multiple elements when helping people through intrapersonal struggles. Stokes suggests, "Pastoral counseling focuses on the promotion of welfare, symptom mitigation, increased coping, positive behavioral transformation, and better relationships with self and others; it considers shifts in a person's spiritual life, values, meanings, and fundamental commitments as vital."[76] Therefore, faith-based, Christian-oriented *Proactive* Pastoral Counseling described in this book shows how biblical thinking is the key to helping others overcome intrapersonal conflict.

Religious Legalism

The spiritual character of the *Church S* example utilizes three views of religious legalism noted by R. C. Sproul: (1) the act of behaving to please oneself; (2) obedience to the externals negating a faithful desire to honor God, the intent of His law, or His Christ; and (3) adding rules to God's law and treating them as divine.[77] Sproul, noting one of his graduate professors, comments, "The essence of Christian theology is grace, and the essence of Christian ethics is gratitude. The legalist isolates the law from the God who gave the law. He is not so much seeking to obey God or honor Christ as he is to obey rules that are devoid of any personal relationship."[78]

In essence, religious legalism goes against God's love as the premise for life and joy, binding others by the rules and regulations laid down by non-spiritual men. Sproul notes, "It's a rote, mechanical form of law-keeping that we call externalism. The legalist focuses only on obeying bare rules, destroying the broader context of God's love and redemption in which He gave His law in the first

---

75. Wilkins, "Educating the Congregation," 17.
76. Stokes, "Heart, Soul, Mind, and Strength," 26.
77. Sproul, "3 Types of Legalism."
78. Sproul, "3 Types of Legalism."

place."⁷⁹ Although Sproul's definition describes the spiritual nature of *Church S* well, Paul's exhortation in 2 Corinthians 3:6 provides a more biblically founded understanding regarding religious legalism and its effects on the hearts and minds of people spiritually. Paul notes, "The letter kills, but the Spirit gives life."

Spirit of the Mind

The spirit of the mind refers to the nature by which man produces his thoughts. In Ephesians 4:17–18, Paul tells the church to no longer walk as the gentiles do, carrying darkened hearts embellished by the futility of their minds. Marshall affirms, "Those who are filled with the Spirit live continually under the influence of the Spirit by letting the Word control them. . . . Being filled with the Spirit is living in the conscious presence of the Lord Jesus Christ, letting his mind, through the Word, dominate everything that is thought and done."⁸⁰

Similarly, in Ephesians 4:22–23, Paul continued, saying, "Lay aside the old self, which is being corrupted in accordance with the lusts of deceit, and . . . be renewed in the *spirit of your mind*" (emphasis mine). Paul urges the church to put on the Spirit of Christ and change the current spirit controlling their minds. In other words, what man fills himself with dictates what spirit operates in his mind, just as adding drugs or alcohol to the body (manufactured spirits) changes one's thinking and behavior.

In the same likeness, inserting God's Word into the mind alters one's behavior, producing a higher sense of spiritual well-being. Thus, one's intrapersonal world becomes ever-changed by the power of the Holy Spirit. Therefore, under the influence of God's Spirit, Christian intrapersonal formation manifests by applying the principles, precepts, and practices found in God's Word, maintaining a godly spirit within one's mind.

---

79. Sproul, "3 Types of Legalism."
80. Marshall and Newheiser, *When Words Matter*, 40.

The Fight for Spiritual Truth

In that light, walking in the Spirit (being led by the Spirit, seeking God's hand in everything) becomes a way of life. In contrast, the "mind of the flesh" promotes walking in wickedness, carnal affections, and spiritual death. Louw says, "True peace of heart and spiritual maturity are found and accomplished in resisting passions, not in satisfying them. There is no peace in the carnal man, in the man given to vain attractions, but there is peace in the fervent and spiritual man."[81] Overall, by connecting the "spirit of the mind" and "religious legalism," one might better understand why those who do not submit to being Spirit-led (*Church S*) behave as they do: rote, mechanical in form, absent of expression or emotion.

Spiritual Discernment

To see God's hand in everything is more than a noble pursuit. Macchia notes, "Spiritual discernment becomes a part of us as we embrace the lifestyle of practicing a preference for God, noticing God in everything, and receiving the hospitality of God in the very places where we are learning to be hospitable to others and even ourselves."[82] Marshall agrees one learns to discern truth from error by making choices according to the commands and principles of Scripture. He describes one's foolishness as replaced with God's wisdom, which is pure, peaceable, gentle, reasonable, merciful, impartial, and sincere.[83]

In the end, without godly discernment, understanding God's will becomes a foolish endeavor for the carnal man. As for spiritual things, "He cannot understand them" (1 Cor 2:14). In that case, spiritual growth purposed for holiness cannot manifest, leaving one's ability to discern spiritual things dormant.

---

81. Louw, "Christian Spirituality of Imperfection," 77.
82. Macchia, *Discerning Life*, 22.
83. Marshall and Newheiser, *When Words Matter*, 61.

Spiritual Discipline

Nothing grants spiritual growth more (other than the Holy Spirit) than spiritual disciplines found in the Holy Bible. Morely asserts, "The Bible is the starting point for all spiritual discipline, for everything that glorifies God, and for all growth and sanctification."[84] Spiritual disciplines include reading the Bible, being silent with God, being in solitude and prayer, and gathering with other Christians regularly for edification and encouragement.

Morley promotes spiritual disciplines as the motivations that change the core reactions of the heart.[85] He says, "They will usher you into a deeper communion with God. You will grow in your knowledge and love for God. You will gain confidence about how to discern His will. You will find yourself yearning, aching, to follow the example of Jesus."[86]

In contrast, spiritual disciplines go against the religious status quo of *Church S*; instead, religious legalism takes precedence, as previously explained (judgmentalism replaced grace). If one does not seek to become influenced by spiritual disciplines, learning stops, spiritual growth ceases, and change never becomes realized (as spiritual death occurs). Marshall explains, "Discipline also includes 'being' disciplined by God through His discipline like a Father to a son."[87]

For *Church S*, personal discipline (or taking responsibility for one's actions oneself) is a thought beyond many parishioner's capability to comprehend. Therefore, without applying spiritual discipline in one's life, life becomes dead, and growth on any level becomes a mere illusion. In short, intrapersonal development does not occur without intentionally growing one's faith in the person and works of Jesus Christ.

---

84. Morley, *Man's Guide*, 42.
85. Morley, *Man's Guide*, 10.
86. Morley, *Man's Guide*, 10.
87. Marshall and Newheiser, *When Words Matter*, 84.

Summary

Spiritual growth is the transformational process where people relocate from self-worship to Christ-centered self-denial.[88] As people grow in Christ, they mature spiritually, becoming more of the design God created them to become. Spiritual growth heightens self-awareness and acts as an essential ingredient for cognitive change.[89] However, every aspect of discernment requires a process, and for believers to grow, a *proactive* pastoral counselor must help them navigate that process.[90] The implication, then, is that Church S is in grave need of PPC.

Instead of acting on everyday emotions to discern circumstances in life, spiritual disciplines integrated into daily routines can help Church S and other believers with the tools they need to live a more spiritually discerned life.[91] Spiritual disciplines, a critical ingredient for spiritual change—combined with the PPC approach—help to manage that process, and intrapersonal struggles might decline (CIF).[92]

For instance, intentionally engaging with God's Word can aid individuals in relearning, understanding, and applying spiritual principles to daily life. By embracing PPC, believers can reduce internal conflict and foster Christian intrapersonal formation.

---

88. Van der Watt, "Mission-Minded Pastoral Theology," 3.
89. White, "Conceptualizing Therapy," 94.
90. Macchia, *Discerning Life*, 170.
91. Eubanks, *How We Relate*, 167.
92. Harris, "Christocentric Discipleship," 45.

— 2 —

Nature, Tenets, and Applications of PPC

PASTORAL COUNSELING IS "FAITH-BASED" biblical counseling that seeks to facilitate Christlike change for all those who struggle spiritually.[1] Intrapersonal conflict, a mental framework of spiritual struggle, requires integrating spiritual disciplines found only in Christianity[2] with pastoral counseling to bring about and address one's internal distress. By combining spiritual conversations and Scripture reading with the integrative perspective of a pastoral counselor, others might become more aware of how to manage cognitive interference, decrease mental struggle, and grow spiritually.[3] Because intrapersonal struggles prevent confidence in others, spiritual growth might drastically fade if pastoral counseling efforts remain reactive instead of proactive.

In that light, this book introduces an innovative approach to cultivating Christian intrapersonal formation in others that

1. Tan, "Dealing with Spiritual Struggles," 311.
2. Whitney, *Spiritual Disciplines*, 8.
3. Stokes, "Heart, Soul, Mind, and Strength," 213.

combines *proactive* pastoral counseling with a Christian worldview, integrating aspects of Christian spirituality, spiritual transformation, and Christian education. While traditional pastoral counseling focuses on intrapersonal renewal through submission to the Holy Spirit's work (and rightly so),[4] *proactive* pastoral counselors emphasize the importance of practicing biblically guided spiritual disciplines to help others make the transformation possible. These counselors actively engage in and foster spiritual conversations, aiming to cultivate deep, heart-to-heart connections. By adopting this *proactive* pastoral counseling approach, there may be a reduction in the increasing demand for spiritual growth among individuals, particularly those living in the likeness of *Church S*.[5]

Intrapersonal Formation and Christianity

The most extraordinary conviction to ever satisfy the core reactions of the human spirit comes from a faithful relationship with Jesus Christ.[6] Christian intrapersonal well-being incorporates a mindset centered around pursuing Christlikeness, while every affection of behavior (internal and external) "upholds spiritual applications that contribute to spiritual formation."[7] The apostle Paul undergirds spiritual formation as receiving "not the spirit of the world, but the Spirit who is from God . . . combining spiritual thoughts with spiritual words" (1 Cor 2:12–13). In essence, spiritual formation results from pursuing the meaning behind the teaching of Jesus Christ (Christianity), which is found only in God's Word, the Holy Bible.

Rhodes suggests applying spiritual disciplines as a mode for growing spiritually. He states, "Spiritual disciplines are the pathway to increasing spiritual discernment."[8] Comparatively, Aadne

---

4. Haykin, *God Who Draws Near*, 63.
5. Macchia, *Discerning Life*, 14.
6. Morley, *Man's Guide*, 10.
7. Whitney, *Spiritual Disciplines*, 4.
8. Rhodes, "Discipling Leadership," 12.

adds, "Intrapersonal well-being results from genuine worship and consistency in submitting oneself to hearing God's Word."[9] Hence, Christian intrapersonal formation occurs by engaging in spiritual disciplines, such as prayer and biblical meditation, guided by the work of the Holy Spirit.[10]

Setran agrees that spiritual disciplines are vital to experiencing the Holy Spirit's work. He says, "Spiritual formation . . . continually forces us to recognize the role of the Holy Spirit in the transformation process, through the Word, and also through such practices as prayer, worship, solitude and silence, fasting, Sabbath-keeping, confession, service, and participation in the liturgical expressions of the local church."[11] Similarly, Eubanks indicates reading the Bible increases intrapersonal growth and one's relationship with God. He stresses, "The Bible constitutes a school of relationship."[12]

Furthermore, Macchia admits the guiding light for Christian spirituality evolves from consistency in living a Christ-centered life.[13] In contrast, White believes that "spiritual disciplines are purposed not for doing but to engage in the process of becoming."[14] Essentially, the power to overcome intrapersonal struggles and encounter spiritual well-being manifests from depending on God to provide spiritual discernment, invoking a spiritual sense of awareness.[15]

Macchia and White agree, adding that spiritual growth and discernment implicate focused attention toward personal levels of self-awareness. Macchia suggests, "When we grow in self-awareness through tools like a spiritual autobiography, our co-cultural experiences, and others, we see greater clarity on how our immediate personal context will either promote or deny the priority

---

9. Aadne, "Radical Discipleship," 87.
10. Setran and Wilhoit, "Christian Education," 542.
11. Setran and Wilhoit, "Christian Education," 542.
12. Eubanks, *How We Relate*, 16.
13. Macchia, *Discerning Life*, 14.
14. White, "Conceptualizing Therapy," 93.
15. White, "Conceptualizing Therapy," 94.

Nature, Tenets, and Applications of PPC

of discernment."[16] However, the apostle Paul confirms, "A natural man does not accept the things of the Spirit of God, for they are foolishness to him; and he cannot understand them, because they are spiritually appraised" (1 Cor 2:14).

Under the construct of Christianity, intrapersonal formation superimposes that while maintaining a relationship with God through Christ is vital for life, God's power (through the Holy Spirit) mobilizes one to change intrapersonally.[17] This is to say that the Holy Spirit is involved in every aspect of salvation and spiritual growth.[18] Morley comments, "God's wisdom is found in Scripture, and it is administered through the Holy Spirit."[19] However, others believe that the responsibility for intrapersonal formation requires more than God's hand.[20]

Hessert notes that God is all-powerful and the sole author of intrapersonal transformation, However, the obligation to embrace a healthy mindset has two sides. He offers, "God may be willing to grant us spiritual insight, but this cannot come unless we are willing to receive it."[21] Clyde Harris acknowledges the presence of the Holy Spirit, who, in every aspect, makes salvation and spiritual growth possible.[22] Van der Watt maintains, "Human existence is inherently relational, and God's power is the key to spiritual maturity."[23] While this commonly connotes that human nature thrives on relationships, those lacking spiritual maturity might struggle to comprehend the core tenets of Christianity, grasp the magnitude of God's power, understand how to seek divine assistance, identify whom to turn to for guidance, or even realize that pastoral counseling is accessible for addressing these concerns.

---

16. Macchia, *Discerning Life*, 141.
17. Van der Watt, "Mission-Minded Pastoral Theology," 3.
18. Harris, "Christocentric Discipleship," 54.
19. Morley, *Man's Guide*, 98.
20. Hessert, *Introduction to Christianity*, 311.
21. Hessert, *Introduction to Christianity*, 311.
22. Harris, "Christocentric Discipleship," 54.
23. Van der Watt, "Mission-Minded Pastoral Theology," 7.

Given this dilemma, a *proactive* spiritual advisor becomes necessary to personally engage others to effect the desired change for the individual and the community.[24] Tan says, "Helping clients deal with their spiritual struggles in constructive ways can facilitate their growth rather than decline."[25] As such, PPC intentionally pursues and engages others for Christ, inspiring Christian intrapersonal formation for all who humble themselves to receive it.

Intrapersonal Formation and Pastoral Counseling

Pastoral counseling inspires intrapersonal formation by combining faith-based therapy with the integrative perspective of the pastoral counselor.[26] When a counselor-client relationship establishes trust, individuals feel safe communicating and forming intrapersonally in Christ.[27] Tan states, "Spiritually integrated psychotherapy . . . facilitates the development of spirituality or spiritual formation into deeper Christlikeness of both the client and therapist."[28] Essentially, pastoral counseling is the mediator that draws others away from intrapersonal conflict toward a closer understanding of themselves through Christ (Christian intrapersonal formation).[29]

As a mediator-in-fact, pastoral counseling engages others with God's Word to help decrease intrapersonal dissonance and increase one's desire for Christlike transformation. Wilkins describes, "Christian counseling in its purest form, is a covenant between a caregiver and a care seeker to labor collaboratively for the possession of the soul (through the power of the Holy Spirit), under the authority of the Word of God, and within a context of accountability and encouragement—for the purpose of the imitation of the Christ."[30] Drawing people toward spiritual maturity

---

24. Dodson, "Assessing Well-Being," 80.
25. Tan, "Dealing with Spiritual Struggles," 313.
26. Dodson, "Assessing Well-Being," 15–16.
27. Ahonle et al., "2023 Revision," 258.
28. Tan, "Dealing with Spiritual Struggles," 311.
29. Stokes, "Heart, Soul, Mind, and Strength," 26.
30. Wilkins, "Educating the Congregation," 17.

NATURE, TENETS, AND APPLICATIONS OF PPC

through implementing biblical principles, such as participating in Spirit-led small group discussions and learning how to apply biblically enhanced spiritual applications in one's life, might best describe the relationship between intrapersonal formation and pastoral counseling.[31]

While intrapersonal formation through a pastoral counselor is available, spiritual growth in Christ ultimately depends on the individual's willingness to pursue it. Setran and Wilhoit highlight alternative pathways for spiritual growth, noting that "the increasing draw of spiritual formation was linked to the expanding reach of postmodern thinking in the academy and the church."[32] Cheng, Green, and Smith observe that "instead of measuring the frequency of engagement in conventional spiritual disciplines or assent to doctrinal belief, they focus on measuring psychological states."[33] This observation suggests a close relationship between assessing psychological states and addressing intrapersonal struggles.

Ultimately, a biblical decision must become available to one's mind to move beyond the errors of one's way. Marshall and Newheiser express, "We learn to discern truth from error and to make choices according to the commands and principles of Scripture."[34] Nevertheless, implementing PPC allows others to safely address spiritual issues not commonly discussed in religiously bound environments or outside of responding to intrapersonal crises, enabling therapy as a spiritual discipline.[35]

At the same time, although pastoral counselors typically attend to spiritual concerns, a pastoral counselor's responsibility involves more, such as dealing with others' mental, physical, and emotional issues. Wilkins states, "The attempt is to assist in the creation of a whole person through spiritual formation and Christlikeness and view the person under the whole person

---

31. Wilkins, "Educating the Congregation," 54.
32. Setran and Wilhoit, "Christian Education," 534.
33. Cheng et al., "Development and Validation," 69.
34. Marshall and Newheiser, *When Words Matter*, 61.
35. White, "Conceptualizing Therapy," 91.

concept as Jesus commands of us."³⁶ He asserts, "Pastoral care for the Christian counselor through self-care and the counselor's care for the congregation becomes soul care with the express goal of spiritual formation."³⁷

Furthermore, Liu and his colleagues noted significant findings in their instrumental case study on intrapersonal formation. They found "intrapersonal growth involved participants' increased reflection of self-identities and personal issues. Participants achieved salient intrapersonal growth across the semester, evidenced by enhanced self-reflection, emotional awareness, and self-concept."³⁸ White adds, "Therapy as a spiritual discipline may help the Church reclaim paths of deep transformation of persons and communities."³⁹ Because intrapersonal conflict permeates internal distress, pastoral counseling must become proactive rather than reactive to help others manage that distress in hopes that Christian intrapersonal formation might become realized in others; thus, there is an alarming need for *Proactive* Pastoral Counseling.

Intrapersonal Formation and Christian Education

Learning to grow spiritually begins when biblical teaching is accepted.⁴⁰ Christian education naturally assumes the teaching position of proper biblical doctrine.⁴¹ In that view, Christian education upholds the pursuit of administering appropriate theology for the spiritual development of others.⁴² PPC also pursues others with a like-minded premise.

Stokes recommends that for the *Christian church* to develop spiritually, fruitfulness must remain its focus, which, empowered

---

36. Wilkins, "Educating the Congregation," 50.
37. Wilkins, "Educating the Congregation," 50.
38. Liu et al., "Counselor Trainees' Personal Growth," 32.
39. White, "Conceptualizing Therapy," 98.
40. Hessert, *Introduction to Christianity*, 311.
41. Harris, "Christocentric Discipleship," 24.
42. Harris, "Christocentric Discipleship," 24.

by the Holy Spirit, replaces all other pursuits. He mentions Christlike teachers and preachers become proactive and intentionally engage their congregants, "equipping them with the decreed Word."[43] Cox believes that "Christian education should academically instill discipleship as the goal of behavior."[44] Comparatively, Macchia recommends applying competent biblical principles and receiving Christian teaching as the catalyst for spiritual movement.[45] Ultimately, the Holy Spirit enables the process and progression of Christian intrapersonal formation.

In other words, spiritual growth is not for the faint of heart, and learning the process is priceless for those who choose the deeper life of humility.[46] Christian doctrine and principles guide others to repentance and faith, producing in them a reverence of worship to God, prompting them to behave in love and dedication in submission to Him.[47] Yet, not everyone knows how to read God's Word or understand its spiritual applications, let alone grasp why living life focused on spiritual disciplines and seeking behavior approved by Christ is essential for overcoming intrapersonal struggle.[48]

Leaf comments that inside the local church, limited learning opportunities for enhancing biblical literacy in adults prove the fragility of adult biblical worldviews and note their decline;[49] when Christian education ceases to work, spiritual blindness increases.[50] Fruitlessness becomes the essence of action in people's hearts, separating them from the ability to discern things spiritually and thereby losing their ability to determine their pastoral counseling needs—producing a decline in spiritual growth.

---

43. Stokes, "Heart, Soul, Mind, and Strength," 81–82.
44. Cox and Peck, "Christian Education," 243.
45. Macchia, *Discerning Life*, 51.
46. Macchia, *Discerning Life*, 51.
47. Stokes, "Heart, Soul, Mind, and Strength," 59.
48. Setran and Wilhoit, "Christian Education," 533.
49. Leaf, "Maintaining a Biblical Worldview," 57–58.
50. Hessert, *Introduction to Christianity*, 148.

Pastoral Counseling and Christian Education

Intrapersonal spiritual growth stagnates in the church when its members choose not to take advantage of pastoral counseling.[51] The members' unwillingness to engage in pastoral counseling limits the church's ability to affect others needing spiritual care. In contrast, pastoral counseling for the flock might become restricted due to the time constraints of the pastor and the lack of lay counselors available to assist in caring for the congregation.

Needless to say, when Christian learning stops, spiritual growth stops, and complacent insight takes hold.[52] For Christian intrapersonal formation, growing stems from pursuing biblical literacy to produce new thinking in hopes others might transform and carry the hope to others. Wilkins says, "Spiritual maturity occurs in the individual that develops discipleship patterns that may be taught for adoption by other believers."[53] Therefore, integrated with PPC, Christian education fashions itself for revamping the thinking process of others, helping them relocate intrapersonally toward Christlikeness while holding to an impetus for providing lay counseling for others.[54]

Globally, pastoral counseling is a Christian education device that teaches others how to rethink the state of their spirituality and reshape their life's narrative at the moment.[55] Leaf agrees, affirming that "thinking is inherent as an intrapersonal act, influencing one's character, values, lifestyle, and behavior."[56] Stokes says, "Pastoral counseling and Christian education that is faithful to God and His word teaches that Christ requires humankind to have a right relationship with Him and with others; as such, this allows for His creation to grow in several different ways with the result

---

51. Wilkins, "Educating the Congregation," 16.
52. Rhodes, "Discipling Leadership," 12.
53. Wilkins, "Educating the Congregation," 71.
54. Stokes, "Heart, Soul, Mind, and Strength," 82.
55. White, "Conceptualizing Therapy," 97.
56. Leaf, "Maintaining a Biblical Worldview," 22.

Nature, Tenets, and Applications of PPC

being a spiritually converted heart and mind."[57] As a result, the cognition process changes, biblical thoughts develop, and new behaviors manifest.

Wilkins admits that Christian education through the integration of pastoral counseling inspires others to think about and sometimes rethink their understanding of Christianity and the enacting spiritual power it beholds.[58] In comparison, Leaf suggests integrating and employing Christian education (among other things) with pastoral counseling to "empower those who experience intrapersonal chaos with the necessary spiritual tools found only in biblical doctrine."[59] One might consider the integration between Christian teaching and PPC as the act of making Christlike disciples.

Harris asserts that disciple-making is essentially the intentional pursuit of a goal.[60] Similarly, Christian education, empowered by a *proactive* pastoral counselor, aims to support individuals who fear addressing their intrapersonal issues, struggle with interpersonal communication, panic in crises, and isolate themselves from others. Stokes emphasizes that "the attention to Christian education in the church is to assist clergy and laity in fostering growth that leads to spiritual maturity and motivates the church's congregation."[61] Unfortunately, believers often fear confronting their intrapersonal issues, revealing the challenges of counseling those who face spiritual turmoil.

Unfortunately, there are reasons why believers fear confronting their intrapersonal issues, exposing the negative side of counseling others who deal with spiritual chaos. Part of the problem pastoral counseling and Christian education encounter involves church members' lack of Christian character, such as emulating a non-Christlike attitude, remaining biblically illiterate, having a spiritual apathy, lacking spiritual awareness, and displaying

---

57. Stokes, "Heart, Soul, Mind, and Strength," 60.
58. Wilkins, "Educating the Congregation," 71.
59. Leaf, "Maintaining a Biblical Worldview," 7.
60. Harris, "Christocentric Discipleship," 78.
61. Stokes, "Heart, Soul, Mind, and Strength," 82.

spiritual blindness.[62] Tan presents a list representing this notion: "The lack of spiritual discernment, church commitment, understanding of the work of the Holy Spirit, and spiritual disciplines."[63] Therefore, pastoral counseling incorporated with Christian education provides an approach that "helps make sense of Christianity and helps others understand how to achieve attitudes and characteristics that emulate Christlikeness."[64]

Interestingly, one must also consider that those needing pastoral counseling might feel unworthy of a righteous pursuit and purposely evade any spiritual formation that requires another person, particularly a faith-based, *proactive* pastoral counselor. Tan notes that counseling measures "need to be done with great sensitivity and caution and care, with much prayer for protection and discernment from the Holy Spirit and informed consent from the client."[65] In contrast, Harris insists, "The Church's central mission is discipleship,"[66] which in its very essence should aim to reach others in that likeness.

Moreover, a *proactive* pastoral counselor might enter into an opportunity to conduct spiritual evaluations simply by engaging in Christian conversations outside the church, premising those conversations on teaching Christianity. This "outside of the walls" approach might inspire individuals to think about forming intrapersonally in Christ without pressure from religious standards. As a general note, PPC does not limit itself to a pastor, per se, but to those willing to provide faith-based counseling such as lay counseling, professional Christian counseling, and the likeness of SM.[67]

Therefore, PPC targets spiritual conflict proactively rather than reactively to inspire Christian intrapersonal growth. The rationale is that Christian spiritual formation occurs in two main ways: (1) surrendering to the Holy Spirit and (2) and adopting a

62. Cheng et al., "Development and Validation," 69.
63. Tan, "Dealing with Spiritual Struggles," 313.
64. Hessert, *Introduction to Christianity*, 329.
65. Tan, "Dealing with Spiritual Struggles," 314.
66. Harris, "Christocentric Discipleship," 78.
67. Haugk, *Stephen Ministry*, 15.

scriptural mindset. In that likeness, intrapersonal conflict diminishes when a spiritually discerning perspective, shaped by spiritual disciplines, governs one's thoughts (2 Cor 10:5).

In summary, PPC intentionally engages others to procure Christian intrapersonal formation. Reactive counseling only provides a temporary fix and inhibits spiritual growth. PPC must become the norm to effect intrapersonal change that lasts.

Theological Foundations in Pastoral Counseling

Under the Holy Spirit's guidance, effective pastoral counseling leverages God's Word to build relationships and help individuals find spiritual well-being and rest in Christ (Matt 11:28–30).[68] As Wilkins notes, "Christian counseling in its purest form is a covenant between a caregiver and a care seeker to labor collaboratively for the possession of the soul, through the power of the Holy Spirit, under the authority of the Word of God."[69] Therefore, pastoral counselors must emphasize Christ's power, the driving force behind intrapersonal change, particularly within the counselor-client relationship.[70] Essentially, the transformative power of God's Word, directed by the Holy Spirit, enables individuals to overcome intrapersonal conflict.[71]

As such, theological foundations in pastoral counseling describe the spiritual direction needed to experience cognitive transformation—an intrapersonal change that comes from the work of God in a person's life (Rom 10:9–10).[72] Likewise, reading books of the Bible (such as John, 1 Timothy, Hebrews, and Deuteronomy) helps one to understand biblical characters who proclaimed God's power through the word of the cross (Deut 18:15–19, 1 Cor 1:18). Similarly, the life and narratives of these noted biblical characters

---

68. Wilkins, "Educating the Congregation," 52.
69. Wilkins, "Educating the Congregation," 17.
70. Van der Watt, "Mission-Minded Pastoral Theology," 7.
71. Stokes, "Heart, Soul, Mind, and Strength," 176.
72. Aadne, "Radical Discipleship," 80.

illustrate that comprehending God's power begins with understanding the beneficence of one's pursuit toward Christlikeness (Matt 5:1–2). Ultimately, when the word of God fills a person's mind, intrapersonal struggles decrease, and Christian intrapersonal formation follows.[73]

God's Word Is All-Sufficient

God's Word is the most righteous, life-giving power that people can ever know (John 6:63). To experience Christian intrapersonal formation, then, is to "listen" to and "uphold" the word of God (theological applications), disciplining oneself toward godliness (1 Tim 4:7), taking "every thought captive to the obedience of Christ" (2 Cor 10:5). Luke records the words that God spoke at the Mount of Transfiguration, saying, "This is My Son. My Chosen One; listen to Him" (Luke 9:35). Thomas Aquinas recognized that "God's plan from all eternity had been to establish the kingdom of Christ" (Isa 46:10).[74] Therefore, Jesus Christ is God's Word in the flesh (John 1:14; grace and truth), who provides the means and spiritual food required for a man to receive Spirit-filled power while on earth (John 6:53–58).[75]

For instance, the book of Hebrews discusses the nature of God's life-giving power and how its purpose is to affect the hearts of man. The author writes, "For the word of God is living and active and sharper than any two-edged sword, and piercing as far as the division of soul and spirit, of both joints and marrow, and able to judge the thoughts and intentions of the heart" (Heb 4:12). Thistelton expresses, "The function and effect of the 'word of God' is to probe and to diagnose the condition of the human heart,

---

73. Tan, "Dealing with Spiritual Struggles," 314.
74. Thomas Aquinas, *Gospel of John*, 11.
75. Thomas Aquinas, *Gospel of John*, 21.

Nature, Tenets, and Applications of PPC

including the self-examination."[76] Therefore, people's words might gain power when they surrender their power to a biblical heart.[77]

Pearl recognizes God's Word as the all-sufficient power for people (2 Tim 3:16–17). He claims the power in man's words originates not from his choice of words but from the power of God Himself. With Hebrews 1:3 as a guide, Pearl notes that in a Christian era of positive speaking (word of faith theology), people believe power comes from speaking the right words. He says, "The text does not say that Jesus upholds all things by the power that comes from his word; it says that his word originates in his power. ... Until God moves in power, our words are powerless."[78] In other words, God's Word, inspired by the Holy Spirit, gives humanity everything it needs to overcome life's struggles, even against all its enemies (Ps 19:7–14).

God's Word Is Holy Spirit Power

Morley contends the Holy Spirit (God's power) is infinitely more powerful than all man's enemies combined,[79] including the enemy of sin (Rom 7:14–25). Moo adds that God's power through the gospel of Christ is something possible for the least of men (2 Cor 12:9), even those who might continuously struggle after salvation (Rom 8:1). He comments, "The gospel unleashes God's power so that people, by embracing it, can be rescued from the disastrous effects of sin, being pronounced 'righteous' in God's sight and having a secure hope for salvation from wrath in the last day."[80] Overall, God's Word and the power of the Holy Spirit provide people with what they need to live, move, and exist (Acts 17:28), and without Him, neither man nor his words would exist or contain any power.

---

76. Thiselton, *Colossians*, 43.
77. Sleeper, *James*, 49.
78. Pearl, *Book of Hebrews*, 3.
79. Morley, *Man's Guide*, 184.
80. Moo, *Epistle to the Romans*, 745.

God's Word Is Life

In the Gospel of John, the writer professes all things came into existence through His Word. He explains, "All things came into being through Him, and apart from Him nothing came into being that has come into being" (John 1:3). At the same time, John reflects on the power of God's Word giving life to men, saying, "In Him was life, and the life was the Light of men" (John 1:4). Carson notes, "John is largely interested in 'light' and 'life' as they relate to salvation: the 'light' is revelation which people may receive in active faith and be saved, the 'life' is either resurrection life or spiritual life that is its foretaste."[81] In short, the Word is the Light of the world (John 8:12).

This "righteous" power (the Light) is the salvation promised by God, who would be born of the Jews (John 4:22). The Bible describes Jesus as the exact representation of godliness, emulating the embodiment of righteousness of earth (Heb 1:3). Through His righteousness, Jesus opens the door for eternal life with God in heaven (John 4:14). He also provides "the way" to receive "Holy Spirit" power in the flesh, providing the means to experience inner peace: Jesus is the peace that passes all understanding (Phil 4:7). To choose a Spirit-filled life in Christ, though, one must first deny himself, take up his cross daily, and follow Jesus (Luke 9:23). Marshall notes, "Only through the willingness to surrender one's life for Jesus will one really gain it, for the person who tries to preserve his life for himself, will ultimately lose it."[82]

For example, the life of the apostle Paul radically changed after his experience with Christ on the Damascus road, an involuntary incursion (see Acts 9).[83] His intrapersonal world had transformed entirely because of his encounter with Christ, causing him to see and hear God differently (Acts 9:18). His internal change was so significant that others, too, recognized his change (Acts 9:20). Comparatively, Paul could not escape the power of Christ,

---

81. Carson, *Gospel According to John*, 119.
82. Marshall, *Gospel of Luke*, 372.
83. Marshall, *Gospel of Luke*, 372.

His words, or the effect of his overall state of being; even more, the spirit of his mind also became renewed (Eph 4:23). Ultimately, the life of Paul changed because of Christ.

God's Word Is Truth

God's Word proclaims there is no other way to receive eternal life with God other than through Jesus, His Son (John 14:6). Jesus declared, "I am the resurrection and the life; he who believes in Me will live even if he dies, and everyone who lives and believes in Me will never die" (John 11:25–26). As described in John 1:17, "For the Law was given through Moses; grace and truth were realized through Jesus Christ." Therefore, one might conclude that whether one hears God's Word voluntarily or involuntarily, "receiving" God's Word is the key to Christian intrapersonal growth and salvation, as prompted in James 1:21.[84]

Garland agrees that intrapersonal formation comes first by hearing the words of Jesus as a command (Luke 9:35). He adds, "The command to listen to Jesus means . . . listen to the revelation of God that comes through Jesus rather than the fickle speculations of public opinion."[85] Essentially, Christlike intrapersonal change occurs when one receives the words spoken by God throughout all the Scriptures (Luke 24:27), particularly in these last days in whom He has spoken through His Son (Heb 1:2).

In other words, without Christ, there can be no spiritual activity inside a person,[86] such as Christian intrapersonal formation. Therefore, one must diligently believe in God's revelation—the person and works of His Son, Jesus Christ—and trust in Him for Christian intrapersonal formation to occur (Rom 12:2). Jesus says, "It is the Spirit who gives life; the flesh profits nothing; the words that I have spoken to you are spirit and are life" (John 6:63).

---

84. White, "Conceptualizing Therapy," 92.
85. Garland, *Luke*, 402.
86. Carson, *Gospel According to John*, 301.

Paul lived on the words of Christ, and from those words, he experienced life. In the book of Romans, Paul mentions, "For the mind set on the flesh is death, but the mind set on the Spirit is life and peace" (Rom 8:6). Taylor notes, "The 'unrighteous,' in contrast to the 'saints,' will not inherit the kingdom of God" (1 Cor 6:11–12).[87] Jesus, the righteousness by which God portrays His grace, displays His desire for all men to be saved and come to the knowledge of the truth (1 Tim 2:4). In other words, Paul chose Christ because he knew no power existed except that power which he beheld in the name of Christ (Phil 2:10).

Ultimately, the Word is the Truth (Christ), giving people power behind their words and hearts.[88] The desire of one's heart to draw closer to understanding the Truth becomes realized from being elevated in His strength, manifesting a renewed heart. Ezekiel illustrates, "I will give you a new heart and put a new spirit within you; I will remove the heart of stone from your flesh and give you a heart of flesh" (Ezek 36:26). Hence, the power of the Truth executed in one's life turns fleshly pursuits toward a Christ-like desire as one's internal activity and focus fixes itself on Christ (Heb 11:2). Nonetheless, becoming more like Christ requires an internal impetus for intrapersonal change.[89]

Change in the heart and mind comes from a willingness to submit to godly discipline, which makes way for God's presence in one's life (1 Tim 4:7).[90] Cockerill notes, "The Son provided the ultimate revelation of God through his high-priestly work, by which he cleansed God's people from sin and thus brought them into God's presence. By so doing, he has become the Pioneer and Perfecter who has initiated and completed the way for the faithful to enter God's presence."[91] Cockerill's use of the term "the way" suggests the Holy Scriptures exist so that people may learn the written words in

---

87. Taylor, *1 Corinthians*, 145.
88. Pearl, *Book of Hebrews*, 3–4.
89. Marshall, *Gospel of Luke*, 267.
90. Marshall, *Gospel of Luke*, 267–68.
91. Cockerill, *Epistle to the Hebrews*, 601.

them and, believing in those words (faith), become renewed in the "spirit of the mind" through Christ (Eph 4:23).

Furthermore, Christian intrapersonal formation—as "a way" to experience Christlikeness—occurs when the cognitive process shifts from ungodly thinking to thinking scripturally (1 Tim 4:6). In contrast, Koester mentions those who do not seek or listen to God's Word do not appear guilty of heinous crimes but are susceptible to drift and neglect.[92] Garland adds, "Those who do not listen and obey will be cut off from the people of God and Salvation."[93] The psalmist says, "But My people did not listen to My voice, and Israel did not obey Me" (Ps 81:11). Concisely, for Christian intrapersonal change to occur, one must seek His Word and become empowered by the Holy Spirit to affect that change—walk by the Spirit (Gal 5:16).[94]

Alternatively, one might argue that intrapersonal change toward Christlikeness also occurs involuntarily, such as with Paul's conversion on the Damascus road and his "revelation of Christ" consummation noted in Acts 9:6. As mentioned, Paul experienced an unplanned spiritual awakening, and his transformation manifested in a new life in Christ—Paul received the ministry of reconciliation (2 Cor 5:14–17). One might then consider that life itself changes, ready or not, when the Holy Spirit is at work in a person's life. For Paul, the power of the Holy Spirit changed his life entirely and became a staple in his preaching ministry. Taylor comments, "Paul's preaching was effective for God's purposes because of the empowerment of the Spirit. The Spirit bore witness to the truth of the message."[95] As such, acting on the "message of truth" paves the way for Christlike intrapersonal growth.[96]

Intentionally filling one's mind with Scripture stimulates new thinking, facilitating a shift from worldly to godly thoughts. Paul wrote to the Christians in Rome, "And do not be conformed

---

92. Koester, *Hebrews*, 312.
93. Garland, *Luke*, 402.
94. Morley, *Man's Guide*, 125.
95. Taylor, *1 Corinthians*, 81.
96. McClendon, *Paul's Spirituality*, 106.

to this world, but be transformed by the renewing of your mind" (Rom 12:2). This raises the question, "How does the mind experience renewal?"

Paul explains in 2 Corinthians 10:5, "We are destroying speculations and every lofty thing raised up against the knowledge of God, and we are taking every thought captive to the obedience of Christ." When a person faithfully receives God's revelation, a transformative power emerges, making even a sinful person a new creation. Therefore, when people choose life and live by God's Word in mind, heart, and spirit (intrapersonal), they experience the fullness of new life, as Moses described to the Israelites in Deuteronomy 30:19–20.

Incidentally, out of all the characters in the Bible, Moses knew firsthand the power of God's word. Moses was the one who instructed the Israelites to place God's Word in their hearts and souls. He expressed the vitality of teaching the words given by God, saying, "You shall teach them to your sons, talking of them when you sit in your house and when you walk along the road and when you lie down and when you rise up. You shall write them on the doorposts of your house and on your gates" (Deut 11:19). Similarly, Paul writes to Timothy, saying, "You will be a good servant of Christ Jesus, constantly nourished on the words of the faith and of the sound doctrine which you have been following" (1 Tim 4:6). As with King Solomon, the teacher, he offers this application: "Apply your heart to discipline and your ears to words of knowledge" (Prov 23:12).

Moreover, shifting from self-thinking to godly formation generates intrapersonal growth and Christlike behavior. Leaf says, "Believers in the Lord Jesus Christ are granted a 'new nature' resulting from the Holy Spirit's regeneration. This new nature enables each believer to develop clearer thinking, a worldview based on the mind of Christ."[97]

Furthermore, Campbell observes, "Individuals are not left to wander on their own, but are called to conduct that is worthy of their Lord and his earthly community. The Spirit lays demands

---

97. Leaf, "Maintaining a Biblical Worldview," 7.

upon each individual completely and concretely in his particular relationships and makes him capable of a new manner of life."[98] One might suggest that pastoral counselors who are proactive rather than reactive might better facilitate this process, yet not being the substance of change themselves.

God's Word Is Christ

Campbell emphasizes body and mind as part of one indissoluble but distinguishable self. He says, "They are affected by being in Christ and should not be flattened to a cipher for the person."[99] In his Pauline letters, Paul emphasized Christianity as faithful action in hearing and applying God's Word (the teachings of Jesus) to one's life. He states, "Continue in the things you have learned and become convinced of, knowing from whom you have learned them, and that from childhood you have known the sacred writings which are able to give you the wisdom that leads to salvation through faith which is in Christ Jesus" (2 Tim 3:14–15). Moreover, Paul proclaims to Timothy that no other word stands the test of time than the words of Jesus (Heb 1:3): Jesus is "the Word" made flesh (John 1:14).

Besides his letters to Timothy, one might consider Paul's commencement to the church in Colossae as the most pertinent instructions for intrapersonal Christlikeness. He says, "Set your mind on the things above, not on the things that are on earth" (Col 3:2). Thiselton writes, "The Christian must keep his or her feet on the ground. Paul wants us to set our minds on things above not so as to avoid the nitty-gritty of everyday life on earth but because looking to the exalted Christ provides the vantage point for seeing our lives."[100] Paul exemplifies that there is no other way to grow in

---

98. Campbell, *Romans*, 329.
99. Campbell, *Romans*, 329.
100. Thiselton, *Colossians*, 88.

Christ than through thinking toward Christ.[101] He prays, "Let the word of Christ richly dwell within you" (Col 3:16).

However, some believed in the transformative power of God to change hearts and minds. Moses urged the people of Israel to engrave, teach, speak, and bind God's Word upon their hearts and souls (Deut 11:18–23). Solomon advised his son to embrace his words and treasure his commandments within him (Prov 2:1). Jesus conveyed His message through a new covenant, stating, "This is My commandment, that you love one another, just as I have loved you" (John 15:12). As individuals read, listen to, and obey God's Word, they gain more transparent understanding of why figures such as Paul, Moses, Solomon, John, David, and many others emphasize and proclaim that nothing in the universe is more life-giving than the power of God's Word (Deut 30:18–19).

Theoretical Foundations in Pastoral Counseling

Theoretical foundations in pastoral counseling, such as Christian Cognitive Therapy (CCT), Cognitive Behavior Therapy (CBT), Integration Perspective (IP), Narrative Therapy (NT), and Rational Emotive Behavior Therapy (REBT), integrate psychology and theology to help believers navigate intrapersonal conflict.[102] Generally, counseling itself subscribes to a platform that allows individuals and couples to achieve their desired change, hoping to reduce conflict from within while increasing positive cognitive functioning. Leins comments, "Most counseling theories or psychotherapy and evidence-based protocols have been about meaningfully reducing symptom severities indicative of identifiable psychopathology and increasing the psychobehavioral functionality of individuals."[103] Although not all counseling theories represent a Christian pursuit, theoretical approaches combined with the presence of theology allow the pastoral counselor to keep cognitive behavioral change

---

101. Campbell, *Romans*, 329.
102. Hinson, "Integrationist Perspective," 454.
103. Leins, "What Makes Pastoral Counseling," 345.

in mind. However, fully understanding the purpose of integrating theoretical approaches within pastoral counseling must also consider the counselor from a religious perspective (Christian). Wilkins states, "The Christian counselor works through the 'Spirit of Truth,' counsels through the 'Counselor,' and is under His guidance and auspices throughout the process."[104] In that process, pastoral counselors employ the appropriate theoretical application depending on a person's intrapersonal needs. Therefore, theoretical applications utilized in a pastoral counseling setting can help people become more self-aware and more accepting of their past, present, and future narratives yet empower them to traverse intrapersonal struggles.[105]

Similarly, Stephen's Ministry (SM), a Christian lay counseling ministry, applies a holistic approach premised on the ministry of presence in Christlikeness, reaching others through proactive lay counseling.[106] In a sense, Stephen's ministers act as church ministers who emulate the characteristics of a church deacon working as a social worker. Syahdin describes, "The word deacon is one of the terms used in the Bible for social service positions in the church."[107] Respectively, Stephen's Ministers personify the actions of lay ministers, whether church deacons or not, reaching out to those hurting from life's daily struggles.

Christian Cognitive Therapy (CCT)

Christian Cognitive Therapy is a form of Christian therapy that focuses on how negative, irrational, extreme, unreasonable, maladaptive, and distorted thinking creates problem feelings such as depression, anger, and other problem behaviors.[108] Like PPC, CCT focuses more specifically on unbiblical thinking as the root of

104. Wilkins, "Educating the Congregation," 46.
105. McDonald and Walker, "Qualitative Research," 46.
106. Haugk, *Stephen Ministry*, 15.
107. Syahdin et al., "Stephen's Ministry Concept," 321.
108. Tan, "Christian Cognitive," 481.

the problem, feelings, and behaviors—CCT acknowledges God's Word as the sole authority for Christian intrapersonal formation.[109] Crabb notes, "Scripture trumps psychological principles even if empirically supported, Scripture is God's inerrant Word, Scripture supersedes psychological opinions, and counselors must commit to a deep understanding of the Scripture."[110] PPC aligns with CCT because they consider problem behavior and feelings with biblical thinking.

Cognitive Behavior Therapy (CBT)

Cognitive Behavior Therapy is a collaborative approach that assumes psychological distress results from disturbances in mental processes, and changing the way one thinks results in a positive, healthy change in behavior and affect.[111] Cheng notes, "Some instruments designed to measure faith formation take a different approach. Instead of measuring the frequency of engagement in conventional spiritual disciples or assent to doctrinal belief, they focus on measuring psychological states."[112] Moorey states, "Helping people change their view of the world is a key component of cognitive behavioral therapies."[113] When comparing PPC against all other theoretical foundations in pastoral counseling, CBT appears to align well for several reasons.

First, CBT addresses cognitive dissonance with a focus on intrapersonal resolve. Second, CBT supports the role of clients in that change occurs both in and outside of therapy. Third, CBT addresses faulty thinking, intending to change it. As such, CBT, like PPC, seeks to elicit insight into the positive results of changing one's self-thoughts and how that leads to changing one's responses and behaviors.[114] In so doing, PPC can perform biblically and still

109. Tan, "Christian Cognitive," 481.
110. Crabb, *Effective Biblical Counseling*, 50–51.
111. Brooks, "Cognitive-Behavior Therapy," 456.
112. Cheng et al., "Development and Validation," 69.
113. Moorey, "Three Ways to Change," 187.
114. Brooks, "Cognitive-Behavior Therapy," 456.

comply with the CBT application even though the theory does not promote intrapersonal wellness in Christ.

Integrative Therapy (IT): Integrative Perspective

Integrative Therapy (IT) encompasses the integration of the Christian faith, the discipline of psychology, the pastoral presence and identity of the pastoral counselor, and one's ability to interchange between faith and psychology in the session.[115] Integrating psychology and Christian belief becomes an art form when applying its faculties, such as the Integrative Perspective (IP), to help bring sense to irrational thinking and behavioral problems to Christians and others.[116] However, like the premise of change within theories such as Cognitive Behavior Therapy, Rational Emotive Behavior Therapy, and Stephen's Ministry, *proactive* pastoral counseling works best when the pastoral counselor displays a personal character that promotes a high sense of spirituality. Tan notes, "Personal or intrapersonal integration, including the spirituality of the integrator or therapist, is the most foundational area of integration."[117]

While the pastoral perspective is critical for procuring cognitive change, IT in a small group setting helps produce interpersonal conversations to reveal and manage inner dialogues that cause continual inner turmoil. Oleś mentions, "Self-critical self-talk might reveal the presence of confrontational dialogues, whereas self-managing self-talk might be more frequent when people engage in integrative dialogues."[118] Still, Harris notes the importance of remembering that "the Holy Spirit is involved in every aspect of salvation and spiritual growth."[119]

As mentioned, an outgoing personality propelled by a highly spirited pastoral counselor provides the best results for those

---

115. Hinson, "Integrationist Perspective," 454.
116. Vanderstelt et al., "Transformational Education," 89.
117. Tan, "Applying Theology," 61.
118. Oleś et al., "Types of Inner Dialogues," 3.
119. Harris, "Christocentric Discipleship," 54.

participating in PPC. White mentions, "Clients are wise to seek therapists who have both willingness and training to actively integrate spirituality into therapy."[120] One might suggest people are more intrapersonally engaged when addressed with a sense of pastoral authority from one who administrates from personal experience with spiritual things.[121] Arguably, people also might experience a higher level of change with someone who emits a unique persona of pastoral experience, identity, and presence. Ultimately, the ideal Integrative Therapist (IT) reflects a genuine attitude and desire for people to grow toward Christlikeness and is readily visible to others.

Additionally, by allowing others to be in the presence of the pastoral counselor, people might learn more about how one overcomes intrapersonal chaos through biblical applications supported by spiritual disciplines.[122] The visual alone helps draw others to a healthier relationship with God.[123] However, overcoming intrapersonal conflict takes more than the presence of a pastoral counselor in action. Scazzero states, "Mature spiritual leadership is forged in the crucible of difficult conversations, the pressure of conflicted relationships, the pain of setbacks, and dark nights of the soul."[124]

Nevertheless, IT relies on the leadership and work of Jesus Christ through the Holy Spirit in the pastoral counselor. Van der Watt adds, "Pastoral caregivers (lay and ordained) guide Christian believers on their journey of spiritual formation to grow into a loving, mature body focused on Christ, its head."[125] Combined, PPC and IT make an excellent proactive approach for eliciting Christian intrapersonal growth in believers.

---

120. White, "Conceptualizing Therapy," 99.
121. Carlson, "Adult Development," 17.
122. Freedman, "Feeling, Thinking and Action," 62.
123. Hinson, "Integrationist Perspective," 454–55.
124. Scazzero, *Emotionally Healthy Leader*, 118.
125. Van der Watt, "Mission-Minded Pastoral Theology," 7.

NATURE, TENETS, AND APPLICATIONS OF PPC

Narrative Therapy

Narrative Therapy (NT) maintains that one's identity is the account of one's life defined by personal stories,[126] also known as selfhood. Bulteau records, "In healthy people, selfhood is strengthened by an adequate balance and coherence between positive internalized self-defining memories (internal referential) and the representation of actual positive feedback resulting from engagement in goal-directed behavior in the environment (external referential)."[127] Moschella notes, "Narrative conversations involve care seekers in examining problems in their social and cultural contexts. This approach avoids conflating the problem with the person and the negative identity conclusions that often result."[128] Hence, CIF and NT might work best when the goal of resolve supports Christian intrapersonal growth and discipleship.

However, this approach also brings a sense of caution for *proactive* pastoral counseling efforts. Although NT can sometimes highlight a "self-help" approach to coping with intrapersonal conflict by reframing the life story of the believer, NT might become incompatible with CIF if it does not first seek a Christlike, discipleship goal in mind. Wilkins affirms, "Discipleship effectively begins when people are challenged to grow spiritually through consistent, practical, and spiritual teachings. Spiritual maturity occurs then in the individual who develops discipleship patterns that may be taught for adoption by other believers."[129] In that light, Christian intrapersonal formation proposes "self-reflection" in Christ, and not just merely an act of "self-reflection" facilitated by a therapeutic approach.

---

126. Jamieson, "Narrative Therapy," 460.
127. Bulteau et al., "Update of Self-Identity," 3.
128. Moschella, "Affect in Narrative Spiritual Care," 152.
129. Wilkins, "Educating the Congregation," 71.

Rational Emotive Behavior Therapy

Rational Emotive Behavior Therapy (REBT), formed by psychologist Albert Ellis in the mid-1950s, constructs itself from a psychotherapeutic approach to help others uncover personal feelings and thoughts while seeking "unconditional self-acceptance."[130] Ellis opened a door for assisting others in understanding how unwholesome self-talk creates intrapersonal conflict, which alludes to actions and behaviors that draw a person away from achieving life-driven goals. Okeke says, "People choose to disturb themselves by adverse circumstances in their lives. The theory (REBT) emphasizes the significant role that thoughts and beliefs about adverse phenomena play in patients' mental and emotional disturbances."[131]

Ellis also believed that by labeling the cause of how cognitive dissonance surfaced, a mental shift to a more positive posture might become the choice of reason, and the newness of intrapersonal conduct might produce new feelings and behaviors.[132] Under the influence of PPC, REBT helps others build hope to achieve new behaviors that have not yet come to life.[133] For instance, one might recognize how replacing low self-esteem with unconditional self-acceptance promotes intrapersonal well-being. Once rational thought surfaces, feelings become bearable, and low self-esteem turns to unconditional self-acceptance, a central theme behind REBT.[134] At this point, the pastoral counselor can proactively implement God's Word (and the Christian worldview) and provide a solid foundation for thinking and creating an intrapersonal life worth living.

---

130. Pramanik and Khuntia, "Decoding," 5.
131. Okeke et al., "Religious Coping Intervention," 3.
132. *Psychology Today*, "Rational Emotive Behavior Therapy."
133. Knight, "Rogerian Therapy," 451.
134. Knight, "Rogerian Therapy," 451.

NATURE, TENETS, AND APPLICATIONS OF PPC

Stephen's Ministry: Stephen's Ministers

Stephen's Ministry (SM) is an organized group of lay leaders within a congregation who intentionally seek others out to provide spiritual care. Like PPC, SM aims to engage others during emotional and cognitive distress to provide aid during one's intrapersonal conflict. SM delivers a sense of hope to others (a ministry of Christian presence) that other clinical therapies do not offer.[135]

Stephen's Ministers meet others in life right where they are rather than being "session-minded."[136] Treatment occurs in the individual's home at a convenient time, in comfortable environments that allow for self-talk and narrative therapy in those who might be hurting, such as in coffee shops, parks, and church building settings. The Stephen's Ministry website defines its goal as, "To provide high-quality, one-to-one, Christ-centered care to people in the congregation and the community experiencing life difficulties."[137]

PPC relates to this approach most because its counseling measures are Christian-minded and involve being proactive rather than reactive. Such efforts include intentionally reaching others right where they are, addressing where a person might hurt most, actively listening and engaging with others, demonstrating genuine care for the other person, expressing positive regard (Rogerian principles),[138] and emphasizing hope through prayer and Scripture to support inner healing.[139]

Most importantly, SM, like PPC, offers a "Ministry of Presence" approach for others to grow toward cognitive Christlikeness. Ultimately, the goal is to implement God's Word to renew the "spirit of the mind" in others while helping people achieve a new intrapersonal perspective about their lives and the new life to come.

135. Haugk, *Stephen Ministry*, 15.
136. Carlson, "Adult Development," 69.
137. Stephen Ministries, "What Is Stephen Ministry?"
138. Pramanik and Khuntia, "Decoding," 5.
139. Garzon, "Lay Counseling," 69.

Conclusion

In life, man's most extreme intrapersonal struggle is his desire to understand how to grow in Christ.[140] At *Church S*, the passion for Christian intrapersonal formation is lacking due to an unwillingness in its believers to submit to PPC and grow. Aadne says, "Finding creative ways to strengthen the communal and relational aspect of discipleship can help churches realize the transformational power within the sphere of covenantal relationships characterized by the grace and unconditional love of the triune God."[141] Therefore, without a PPC program addressing the need for Christian intrapersonal formation, *Church S* might stagnate and lose sight of future spiritual growth.

However, by implementing a *proactive* pastoral counseling program, *Church S* might come to learn, discern, and understand spiritual things by integrating theological and psychological therapeutics. Blunt suggests, "An understanding of embodied cognition can help us to understand the application of biblical principles in our lives and to facilitate psychological counseling."[142] Ortberg notes, "The spiritual life begins with paying attention to our thoughts."[143]

Klaus Issler suggests, "To narrow our gaps and become more like Jesus, we need to recognize the important role that core beliefs hold in our character, from which flow our thoughts and actions."[144] In His temptation, Jesus illustrates the perfect response: "It is written, 'Man shall not live on bread alone, but on every word that proceeds out of the mouth of God'" (Matt 4:4).

In that light, one might better understand the nature of pastoral counseling, that holding to a proactive approach with a scripturally minded impetus might spiritually affect others toward Christian intrapersonal formation. Haykin asserts, "The Christian Scriptures are the primary text for Christian spirituality. We don't

---

140. Rice, "Subject Matter Conversations."
141. Aadne, "Radical Discipleship," 93.
142. Brunt, "Role of Embodied Cognition," 242.
143. Ortberg, *Me I Want to Be*, 91.
144. Issler, *Living in the Life*, 28.

Nature, Tenets, and Applications of PPC

form our personal spiritual lives out of a random assemblage of favorite texts in combination with individual circumstances; the Holy Spirit forms us following the text of the Holy Scriptures."[145] In other words, Christian intrapersonal growth takes time while the Holy Spirit inwardly works His will in man.[146]

Spurgeon mentions spiritual faculties compose his inner being for a purpose. He notes, "My spiritual faculties, and my inner life, are my battle axe and weapons of war."[147] Although one must employ sound doctrine to overcome spiritual conflict intrapersonally, Christian intrapersonal formation intentionally fashions, formulates, engages, confronts, directs, navigates, and manages how one's cognition becomes analyzed by the individual.

For example, Schema and Thema provide one approach for understanding how to interpret intrapersonal conflict.[148] One might identify PPC as the composition of each theory's best practices—eclecticism, distinguished only by its proactive Christian nature. Essentially, PPC promotes Christian intrapersonal formation in the individual, holding to new life through the eyes of God's Word.

God's Word offers life-giving hope, providing more than just a sense of "Holy Spirit" power or the act of receiving Christ's saving grace: for believers, God's Word is life itself (John 6:63). Replacing worldly thinking with Scripture allows God's heart and mind to govern the believer's heart, mind, and spirit (Rom 12:2). By briefly considering theoretical applications such as CBT, CCT, IT, NT, REBT, and SM, a broader understanding of intrapersonal matters emerges. Therefore, to encourage Christian intrapersonal growth, a pastoral counselor must proactively engage with others and help them align their mindset with biblical thinking under the influence of the Holy Spirit.

---

145. Haykin, *God Who Draws Near*, 63.
146. Rhodes, "Discipling Leadership," 12.
147. Spurgeon, *Lectures to My Students*, 8.
148. Maddix, "Spiritual Formation," ch. 7.

— 3 —

How *Proactive* Pastoral Counseling Works

PASTORAL COUNSELING PROVIDES A platform for faith-based pastors and pastoral counselors to empower those who struggle with spiritual conflict with the gospel of Jesus Christ.[1] In other words, "The pastor's focus in 'counseling' is the message of the cross; the foremost priority of his work is articulating that message well."[2] Essentially, pastors and pastoral counselors seek to encourage those experiencing brokenness in their minds and hearts to pursue spiritual disciplines, such as reading the Bible, memorizing Scripture, and applying biblical thinking. In that light, believers may undergo a transformative three-fold experience: heightened self-awareness in Christ, reduced intrapersonal conflict, and Christian Intrapersonal Formation.

From this perspective, Christian therapy aligns with pastoral counseling not as a reactive measure to address intrapersonal conflicts per se but as a *proactive* approach to aid believers in

1. McMinn and Campbell, *Integrative Psychotherapy*, abstract.
2. Leins, "What Makes Pastoral Counseling," 344.

understanding how spiritual disciplines, guided by the Holy Spirit, foster a journey toward Christlikeness. Tan emphasizes, "From a Christian perspective, prayerful dependence on the Holy Spirit is crucial and essential to effectively conduct Christian therapy and to help clients deal with spiritual issues, including spiritual struggles in therapy, in a constructive way that leads to growth and spiritual formation into deeper Christlikeness."[3]

Fundamentally, pastoral counseling encourages individuals to transition from a secular to a biblical vocabulary, promoting a consistent focus on God in every aspect of life and enhancing Christian intrapersonal formation. Macchia underscores that "the spiritual discipline of noticing God is central to our formation into Christlikeness."[4] In his Gospel, Luke highlights Jesus' teaching: "If anyone wishes to come after me, he must deny himself, take up his cross daily, and follow me" (Luke 9:23).

In contrast, Leaf says, "Since every person's worldview is continually being modified, it becomes ever more challenging for believers to keep their thinking consistent with Scripture."[5] One might agree then that intentionally filling one's mind with God's Word produces biblical thinking and helps believers maintain their Christian worldview—a biblical life is a "Spirit-filled" life (John 6:63). By changing the words used for cognitive processing, past and present life narratives change, internal concepts change, ideas readjust, and new life commitments become highlighted.

Morley asserts, "The Bible is the foundation for all spiritual disciplines, the source of everything that glorifies God, and the basis for all growth and sanctification."[6] Leaf explains, "A believer's transformed cognitive faculties enable them to develop an organized and interconnected set of beliefs about life grounded in a committed trust in the person and message of Jesus Christ as revealed in the Bible."[7] Moreover, when Christ drives intrapersonal

3. Tan, "Dealing with Spiritual Struggles," 314.
4. Macchia, *Discerning Life*, 112.
5. Leaf, "Maintaining a Biblical Worldview," 7.
6. Morley, *Man's Guide*, 42.
7. Leaf, "Maintaining a Biblical Worldview," 51.

change, core beliefs are transformed, leading to an increased desire to trust and follow God.

In perspective, PPC's applications, faculties, administrations, and guidance offer the spiritual tools and sources needed for others to gain control of their intrapersonal world. Marshall highlights, "Those who are filled with the Spirit live continually under the influence of the Spirit by letting the Word control them. . . . Being filled with the Spirit is living in the conscious presence of the Lord Jesus Christ, letting his mind, through the Word, dominate everything that is thought and done."[8] However, because people are prone to walking in the flesh, pastoral counseling often occurs in response to someone presently hurting (or in crisis mode) or from something preexisting that causes continual inner turmoil.

Nonetheless, when individuals grappling with intrapersonal turmoil finally seek counseling, the steps toward finding a resolution become significantly more effective. At this point, integrating psychology and behavioral sciences can be highly beneficial for fostering hope in the individuals and sustaining the counselor-client relationship. Stokes advocates for pastoral counseling as an approach that addresses mental health care by combining insights from psychology and the behavioral sciences with spirituality, religion, and theology.[9] Realistically, hope restores faith in the ability to change, while the Holy Spirit exacts and produces longevity for that change."[10]

With the aforementioned in mind, this book introduces a new method of pastoral counseling that intentionally draws others out of their intrapersonal world and applies practical, biblical insights for cultivating cognitive resolve. Instead of administering pastoral counseling from a reactive state, the pastoral counselor proactively engages others to address intrapersonal issues and concerns not often discussed, meeting others right where they are. This CIT and new integrative approach is called *Proactive* Pastoral Counseling.

---

8. Marshall and Newheiser, *When Words Matter*, 40.
9. Stokes, "Heart, Soul, Mind, and Strength," 26.
10. Stokes, "Heart, Soul, Mind, and Strength," 135.

Proactive Pastoral Counseling (PPC)— An Integrative Approach

Proactive Pastoral Counseling (PPC) is an integrative approach to Christian therapy that integrates the pastoral counselor's identity, combining pastoral experience, education, and presence (Integrative Perspective) with theoretical models such as CCT, CBT, and NT. Unlike traditional methods that respond to crises when they occur, PPC actively seeks out believers experiencing intrapersonal conflict, addressing these issues before they escalate. Grounded in a Christian worldview and bolstered by Christian Education (CE), PPC endeavors to guide individuals out of their current cognitive patterns, helping to reshape their thought processes by shifting their spiritual focus toward biblical thinking. Cultivating biblical thinking involves self-reflection "in Christ," which, through the inspiration of God's Word, nurtures Christian Intrapersonal Formation.[11]

For example, the apostle Paul was an "ambassador for Christ" who preached God's Word as the "substance of change" (2 Cor 5:19). Paul shared God's Word adamantly, proclaiming life with God through the "ministry of reconciliation" and "the word of reconciliation" (2 Cor 5:18–19). He preached, "Be reconciled to God" (2 Cor 5:20) so Christ might become revealed as the object of change, and become effectual "doers of the word" (Jas 1:22). Cox notes, "It is relatively rare that Christian education for adults organically incorporates discipleship within academic and professional programs, much less make discipleship the guiding conceptual framework."[12]

Like Paul, PPC interacts with others to become more Scripture-minded, enabling believers to understand themselves more clearly. In one sense, PPC guides and helps others understand how to implement biblical thinking in one's mind to function in Christ-likeness. In so doing, one can hope for intrapersonal conflict to decrease, as applying God's Word to one's intrapersonal world in

---

11. Setran and Wilhoit, "Christian Education," 542.
12. Cox and Peck, "Christian Education," 246.

the form of Christian education brings about Christian intrapersonal formation.[13]

PPC also addresses one's intrapersonal culture—core beliefs that dictate social behavior and normalities found in human societies—to help prevent future cognitive disruptions.[14] For example, Christian Cognitive Therapy (CCT), aligned with Christian Education, helps PPC cultivate a safe space[15] to discuss individual problem issues such as depression, anger, and irrational thinking that creates maladaptive feelings. While doing so, PPC hopes to teach others how to display heartfelt acceptance toward oneself and emotional openness toward others.

The apostle Paul writes, "Be kind to one another, tenderhearted, forgiving each other, just as God in Christ also has forgiven you" (Eph 4:32). The Gospel of Mark exposes how one should apply love in life as a whole: "Love your neighbor as yourself" (Mark 12:31). Timoney writes, "The capacity to accept oneself and one's limitations when encountering others with different perspectives, abilities, and worldviews requires an openness to learn from others and an openness to see the potential for growth within oneself."[16] Therefore, the advantage of implementing *Proactive* Pastoral Counseling is that it enhances individuals' capacity to navigate and overcome intrapersonal conflicts while fostering their journey toward Christian intrapersonal formation.

Moreover, PPC counseling intensifies one's ability to communicate interpersonally, strengthens a person's overall health, and offers a lasting narrative. Stokes illustrates, "Narrative, as practiced in pastoral counseling, frames the Word of God into the context of a caring alliance built on faith."[17] Acting proactively (PPC), the pastoral counselor can help build a foundation of care and trust with others to help stabilize one's ability to recognize, accept, and

---

13. Setran and Wilhoit, "Christian Education," 542.
14. Leaf, "Maintaining a Biblical Worldview," 146.
15. Haugk, *Stephen Ministry*, 15.
16. Timoney, "Identifying the Core Components," 4.
17. Stokes, "Heart, Soul, Mind, and Strength," 102.

manage one's intrapersonal world biblically.[18] The following methodology helps to explain that undertaking.

Setting

Proactive Pastoral Counseling is a method of Christlike therapeutics that decreases intrapersonal conflict while procuring Christian intrapersonal formation in believers.[19] In fostering a Christlike environment within a small group, CIF seeks to draw believers out of their present cognitive state while helping them reengage their intrapersonal world with a renewed "spirit of the mind" (Eph 4:23). Through the implementation of *proactive* pastoral counseling measures, such as the pastoral counselor's IP, CIF inspires fellowship with other participants, increases biblical literacy and self-esteem, decreases intrapersonal chaos, enhances interpersonal communication with others, and allows participants to understand in more depth any intrapersonal activity in themselves that might bring light to one's inward strife. Likewise, incorporating the IP and guidance of the pastoral counselor (PPC), CIF can become the conduit for self-reflection[20] in Christ for believers in a nonjudgmental atmosphere.

With this impetus, the CIF-designed small group suggests hosting no more than six active believers who meet for at least three hours once a week (or more, depending upon group dynamics) until the problem discussed finds a biblical resolution. The rationale is that larger groups can impede the transparency and depth of intrapersonal conversations. The small group format does not imply that CIF is ineffective in more extensive settings; instead, it underscores that PPC optimizes itself for faith-based counseling that is intimate, personal, engaging, and transformative—an environment more readily achieved in smaller groups. Smaller groups

---

18. Wilkins, "Educating the Congregation," 51.
19. Van der Watt, "Mission-Minded Pastoral Theology," 3.
20. Liu et al., "Counselor Trainees' Personal Growth," 15.

foster emotional openness among participants while ensuring confidentiality for their life narratives and experiences.[21]

Small group locations may also vary, including church rooms, home gatherings, or even a park visit on a pleasant day to enhance comfort and inspiration. At the end of each session, the *proactive pastoral counselor* prompts the CIF small group with a final discussion to address any unresolved questions or identify new insights or personal changes. Through direct personal engagement, PPC fosters Christian intrapersonal formation in believers by intentionally addressing and transforming intrapersonal conflicts with biblical thinking.

Detailed Intervention Plan: Overview

Proactive Pastoral Counseling addresses cognitive challenges that prevent believers from forming healthy relationships and engaging in Christlike ministry. By fostering transformation through CIF, PPC aims to help believers deepen their relationship with Christ while learning to reduce intrapersonal conflict. PPC seeks to empower individuals to become the people God intended them to be, enabling them to maintain healthy relationships, interact positively with their community, and guide others toward Christlikeness. The goal is to enhance believers' ability to approach themselves and others with a Christlike mindset, as described in Philippians 2:1–5.[22] Utilizing the pastoral counselor's IP, the CIF training program helps participants understand that Christlike transformation in themselves and others is achievable.

Implementation of Intervention Design

To implement the plan, the pastoral counselor begins part one of week one of the CIF training course by introducing pastoral counseling and explaining the nature and goal of the counselor-client

---

21. Haugk, *Stephen Ministry*, 15.
22. Cheng et al., "Development and Validation," 83.

How Proactive Pastoral Counseling Works

session. The pastoral counselor explains the relationship between participant and counselor, the purpose and efficacy of the course, and how PPC can help others grow in Christ intrapersonally. Elevating one's biblical literacy, increasing one's level of spiritual discernment, decreasing intrapersonal conflict in oneself, and improving one's ability to communicate interpersonally are part of PPC's growing process and intended focus.

The pastoral counselor then introduces and defines PPC, explaining its capability to assist individuals in navigating intrapersonal struggles. In this context, Christian Intrapersonal Formation—a four-step training program—employs biblical thinking to help individuals overcome intrapersonal conflicts. The CIF four-step training program entails the following process:

1. *Identify the Nature of the Believer's Intrapersonal Conflict*: Establish the need for intervention by understanding the specific intrapersonal issues faced by the believer.
2. *Encourage Scripture Reading and Prayer*: Promote these practices to refocus the believer's thoughts and emotions.
3. *Provide a Biblical Application*: Apply Scripture to address the believer's needs.
4. *Implement Theoretical Applications*: Utilize relevant theoretical approaches to address any irrational thinking that hinders the believer from adopting a biblical mindset (e.g., CBT, CCT, REBT).

PPC suggests that without biblical thinking, one might suffer from continuous personal struggle and experience a lack of spiritual rest.[23]

In perspective, those who are unable to overcome internal turmoil create unhealthy people, and unhealthy people create unhealthy churches. Tozer explains, "The health of the Church is in direct proportion to the health of each Christian. If the Church is to grow and be healthy, the individual Christians comprising

---

23. Leaf, "Maintaining a Biblical Worldview," 50.

the Church must grow spiritually."[24] Therefore, the goal of the *proactive* pastoral counselor is to engage and discuss the areas of intrapersonal conflict chosen among the group, hoping to elicit any desired change in the participants throughout the safety of the CIF training course.

Next, the pastoral counselor introduces and defines the IP and its purpose within the course setting. The IP[25] combines the pastoral counselor's education, experience, identity, and pastoral presence to help individuals navigate cognitive struggles. These struggles may arise from various issues, such as a lack of spiritual leadership, spiritual apathy among believers, lack of faith (trust in God), spiritual oppression, and communication difficulties. In addressing these areas, the IP also tackles other related issues, including low self-esteem, fear of judgment and rejection, feelings of unworthiness and brokenness, pride, selfishness, self-centeredness, and a lack of self-worth. As a reminder, the goal is to apply a biblical approach to foster Christian intrapersonal formation.

Finally, as each participant grows in their understanding of the nature and purpose of pastoral counseling, the pastoral counselor outlines the four steps involved in participating in the CIF small group. First, the group collectively identifies the issues within the church setting that will serve as the focus for weekly discussions. Second, participants seek relevant Scripture each week to help address their intrapersonal conflicts related to the identified issues. Third, each participant evaluates the selected Scripture to understand its spiritual application and apply it to their life. Fourth, theoretical approaches such as CCT, CBT, and REBT are employed to identify and address any irrational or negative thinking that may hinder biblical thinking. This process fosters further discussion and helps participants shift from self-centered to biblical thinking, strengthening their ability to overcome intrapersonal struggles.

Ultimately, PPC focuses on helping others realize that intrapersonal conflict decreases when biblical thinking becomes the

---

24. Tozer, *Crucified Life*, 13.
25. White, "Conceptualizing Therapy," 99.

bedrock of processing one's thoughts. Likewise, Christian intrapersonal formation elevates in people when biblical thinking becomes the way one's intrapersonal world processes daily thought.[26] In other words, healing occurs in one's inner world when a Christlike focus prevails in the hearts of those who struggle to cope with their hurt.[27]

CIF Training Course Intervention Plan

In the second part of week one, the CIF training course begins with a group exercise called "Pass the Phrase." The pastoral counselor starts by writing an eight-to-ten-word phrase on a piece of paper without showing it to anyone. With the words written face down, the pastoral counselor whispers them to the first participant and instructs them to "pass the phrase" to the next person in the group. This process continues until the last participant has heard the phrase. At the end, the final participant reveals the phrase they heard to the group. The exercise aims to determine whether the final phrase matches the original one shared by the pastoral counselor, highlighting the importance of clear and accurate communication.

Suppose each participant accurately conveys the eight-to-ten-word phrase whispered by the pastoral counselor. In that case, the phrase revealed by the last person should match the original words written on the paper. However, if the final phrase does not match the original, it indicates that someone along the line either miscommunicated or misheard it, leading to miscommunication. During this process, participants might reflect on the following:

- "Are the words I heard the exact words written on the paper?"
- "Should I believe what I hear is correct?"
- "The only thing I know is what I've been told. How will I know if what I hear is the truth?"
- "Will I believe what I hear?"

26. Leaf, "Maintaining a Biblical Worldview," 7.
27. Stokes, "Heart, Soul, Mind, and Strength," 92–93.

- "Oh no, I hope I'm not the one who messes this up!"

The "Pass the Phrase" exercise illustrates how thoughts and beliefs are influenced by how one listens and what they ultimately choose to believe. Timoney emphasizes, "What one hears significantly impacts a Christian's thoughts, feelings, and behaviors."[28] As noted in PPC, words determine how personal conclusions about oneself, such as one's life narrative, formulate.

In contrast, each participant might also better understand why it is critical to process thought and one's life narrative through Scripture (Prov 3:5–7)—biblical thinking is the cognitive process that provides one's intrapersonal world to function rationally. Therefore, the "Pass the Phrase" exercise highlights that what one hears intrapersonally (inner dialogue, self-talk) does not always represent the truth, nor can one always believe in the words one uses when conversing with oneself, mainly if words and beliefs do not stem from biblical thinking.

Overall, the exercise hopes to inspire each participant to look inside themselves, evaluate how they produce thought, and examine what they might say about themselves and others. For example, some may ask, "Is what I say about myself true?" and "How do I think about myself?" Ideally, the exercise intends to provoke new thoughts and awareness in each participant, alluding that the stories, phrases, and words people hear do not always represent the truth, extending even to one's internal dialogues and self-talk conversations with oneself.

Oleś says, "Self-talk seems to occur in reaction to or anticipation of specific events or circumstances, whereas inner dialogue involves more reflective or contemplative kinds of intrapersonal communication."[29] In that light, assessing what and how one thinks might help others reframe what they believe and how they feel—to decrease intrapersonal conflict and provide a means for finding a cognitive resolution much sooner.[30]

28. Timoney, "Identifying the Core Components," 11.
29. Oleś et al., "Types of Inner Dialogues," 2.
30. White, "Conceptualizing Therapy," 97.

Ultimately, our internal dialogues about personal confidence, fears of judgment, and self-perception come to light. Becoming aware of these intrapersonal conversations and discerning where truth resides enables us to make informed decisions about our inner demeanor and spiritual well-being. When self-awareness heightens and areas of internal conflict need addressing, a *proactive* pastoral counselor can help guide the transition to a more desired state, offering insights to inspire Christlike transformation.[31] As Macchia states, "The way of Jesus is our continual objective. But it takes daily practice to live life open-handedly in submission to the Father, to learn how to breathe deep, receive humbly, release indiscriminately, and respond intentionally in the power of the Spirit."[32] Once the exercise concludes, the pastoral counselor proceeds with evaluating the session.

Class Assessment

In the class assessment stage in part two of week one, the group takes a few moments to decide on the areas of internal strife most hindering Christian intrapersonal formation. For example, five areas of concern within the CIF small group reflect the lack of spiritual leadership within *Church S*, spiritual apathy among believers, lack of faith (trust in God) within the church, spiritual oppression toward others, and the inability of believers at *Church S* to communicate (lack of communication) interpersonally with each other. Each week, one topic highlights the discussion area while each participant comes closer to finding an intrapersonal resolution per the problem discussed each week.

Next, the pastoral counselor employs a blended tool to measure where participants stand intrapersonally within themselves and as believers. Distributed to each participant are the "Four Marks of a Disciple" questionnaire, a "feelings" vocabulary list, and a theological assessment to determine one's relationship with

---

31. Harris, "Christocentric Discipleship," 88.
32. Macchia, *Discerning Life*, 153.

Christ using the letters of the alphabet. While each participant undergoes the evaluation in class, the pastoral counselor takes aside one person at a time and performs a one-on-one interview until all assessments and interviews have finished. Each interview should take no more than five to ten minutes.

After conducting the interviews and before the class concludes in the first week, the *proactive* pastoral counselor prepares the group for the upcoming study by reminding them of the problem chosen for investigation in the second week. The interval between classes allows each participant to delve into Scripture, explore spiritual applications, and identify irrational thoughts that may hinder their use of Scripture for intrapersonal resolution. Although each CIF class confronts the primary problem for discussion, the PPC process remains consistent from weeks two through six, regardless of how long it takes to complete the class curriculum. In that light, the following four steps outline the PPC process for achieving Christian intrapersonal formation.

CIF Step 1: Address the Problem

In weeks two through six, the class begins by "passing the phrase" around the group. As mentioned, this exercise prompts each participant to focus on one's cognitive process and get in tune as a group. After the exercise, the pastoral counselor begins the small group conversation by defining the nature of the problem. In this case, week two starts by discussing intrapersonal conflict caused by the "Lack of Spiritual Leadership" at *Church S*. As the discussion develops, each participant adds to the debate by responding with a personal narrative of how the problem directly relates to each believer and why it is a problem to them—emotional and cognitive disruptions.

Eventually, trust in the group develops, and participants begin to crosstalk more steadily—interpersonal communication helps reveal the intrapersonal world of the participants involved in the discussion.[33] As each believer increases participation in the conversation, others gain new perspectives on their life narratives by hearing the perceptions of others with the same problem. The hope is that each group member might learn how to reframe intrapersonal conflict as it relates directly to their life narrative to understand better how to manage and overcome inner chaos in the present and the future.

To help each group member better understand the details of the problem, the pastoral counselor guides each participant's narrative (Integrative Perspective) toward biblical thinking, gently addressing any emotional wounds along the way. Depending on the group's energy and attitude, the pastoral counselor may probe deeper into an individual's narrative to uncover the depth of their struggle or maintain a broader group perspective in the discussion. Suppose the conversation does not engage participants or someone has an adverse reaction. In that case, it may be appropriate to suggest discussing the topic further in a future session, perhaps privately or in a smaller group. Regardless, each participant takes note of the insights or essential comments from the discussion, and the pastoral counselor records any observations crucial for helping others understand the problem (personal narrative) more clearly.

CIF Step 2: Seek Scripture

After the group has had time to examine the problem during the week, turning to Scripture next becomes most important for learning how to cope better. Depending upon the nature of the concern and the level of need for intervention each week, the pastoral counselor might provide some relative Scripture to initiate intrapersonal and interpersonal movement within the group.

For example, because each believer's issues entail identity, such as experiencing a lack of confidence, personal rejection, and religious judgment from others, the pastoral counselor might consider turning to Scripture on God's lovingkindness that can help

---

33. Liu et al., "Counselor Trainees' Personal Growth," 14.

one begin thinking biblically. This approach might help one better understand intrapersonal conflict regarding rejection and identity struggles. The Psalms provide deep encouragement for those who struggle with confidence, self-identity, and trust, as do many stories throughout the Bible, providing spiritual food to help others grow toward Christlikeness.

In this example, one might consider discussing Psalm 118, which highlights God's enduring love and the importance of taking refuge in the Lord rather than trusting in human strength (Ps 118:8). By reflecting on such verses, participants can discover alternative ways of thinking—contrasting personal viewpoints with biblical perspectives. This process enables believers to view themselves through God's love, leading to a transformed self-perception. As participants increasingly turn to Scripture to navigate intrapersonal conflicts and incorporate Christian principles to manage their internal dialogue, they may experience reduced cognitive dissonance and foster Christian Intrapersonal Formation.[34] To facilitate this transformation, the pastoral counselor moves to help explain the Scripture's purpose and application for each participant.

CIF Step 3: Biblical Application

God desires all men "to be saved and to come to the knowledge of the truth" (1 Tim 2:4).

As such, for things to change in one's intrapersonal world, the participant must submit to the control of biblical thinking and its application, believe in the Scripture, and act on it (look, think, act).[35] Incidentally, this construct defines *Proactive* Pastoral Counseling and how Christian intrapersonal formation develops in the believer.

---

34. Wilkins, "Educating the Congregation," 71.
35. Stringer and Aragón, *Action Research*, 123.

Applying the spiritual principle from Psalm 118:8 involves recognizing how our thoughts influence our behavior.[36] Paul encourages believers to "take every thought captive to the obedience of Christ" (2 Cor 10:5), acknowledging that through Christ, God supplies all the identity one could ever need and offers an immense sense of trust and security. We appreciate God's power and lovingkindness by shifting our perspective to think biblically rather than secularly. He values each person profoundly, considering them "more valuable than many sparrows" (Matt 10:31). This biblical understanding enhances one's sense of worth and fosters new thinking, cultivating a renewed identity and confidence in Christ.

In the present case, one way to apply the spiritual application within Psalm 118:8 is to understand how thoughts control how one behaves. With this in mind, Paul recommends believers to take "every thought captive to the obedience of Christ" (2 Cor 10:5), knowing that God, through Christ, provides all the identity one could ever imagine needing, let alone resting in the trust God provides so mightily. To only think biblically instead of secularly about the power and lovingkindness of God and that He considers each person more valuable than many sparrows magnifies the sense of one's worth and creates new thinking, giving a person a new identity and confidence in Christ.

Furthermore, submitting one's thinking to Christ gives that person not only a sense of new life but also gives one's life a new meaning altogether (2 Cor 5:17). Once one's intrapersonal world becomes anew from biblical thinking, Christian intrapersonal formation becomes the norm and manifests in the daily walk of humility in front of the Lord. James writes, "In humility receive the word implanted, which is able to save [you]" (Jas 1:21).

Learning and applying the spiritual principles in Scripture is intended to help individuals overcome intrapersonal struggles. Recognizing the transformative power of engaging with Scripture is crucial for developing empowered thinking—biblical thinking, which the Holy Spirit guides, brings peace and relief from internal conflicts (Matt 11:28–30). Applying biblical teachings from

---

36. Timoney, "Identifying the Core Components," 11.

Scripture involves daily submission to spiritual disciplines like prayer and godly meditation. Concurrently, the Holy Spirit works within believers' hearts and minds, guiding their walk in Christ and reducing the likelihood of future inner turmoil.[37]

CIF Step 4: Theoretical Application

In the final step, the pastoral counselor assesses the conversations relayed throughout the class and provides the group with additional insights motivated by a theoretical perspective. Applying the appropriate therapeutic applications (previously mentioned), the pastoral counselor asks, "Are there any irrational thoughts or adverse thinking that stop you from thinking biblically?" The pastoral counselor then redirects the group to understand the purpose of the illustration from the "Pass the Phrase" exercise at the beginning of the class.

The lesson in step 4 hopes for others to grasp that what a person hears and tells themselves do not always represent the truth, especially when looking intrapersonally, and they can experience change by becoming aware of who they are in Christ. By integrating the pastoral counselor's perspective and counseling therapies, such as CCT and NT, the *proactive* pastoral counselor might bring a sense of renewal to the story and narratives of each participant and procure Christian intrapersonal formation.

Near the end of each class, each participant reflects on the class discussion by providing a final journal entry. At the same time, the pastoral counselor briefs the group on the problem for the following week and the study to come—each participant notes any new intrapersonal movement or insights the individual or group might discuss to prepare for the next week. Writing down all observations and pertinent comments in the reflection journal becomes part of the study—steps 1 through 4 are repeated for weeks two through six. The course ends once all assessments, interviews, and journals have recorded the data to complete the research.

37. Harris, "Christocentric Discipleship," 54.

Conclusion

The issue at *Church S* arises from believers' reluctance to engage in *Proactive* Pastoral Counseling and confront the persistent spiritual challenges that impede their Christian intrapersonal growth. The problems faced by the congregation include a lack of spiritual leadership, insufficient trust in God, poor interpersonal communication skills, experiences of spiritual oppression, and a general sense of spiritual apathy. PPC exists to help believers overcome intrapersonal conflict through a structured four-step process. This process involves (1) identifying the problem, (2) seeking guidance from Scripture, (3) applying the spiritual principles found in Scripture, and (4) utilizing therapeutic approaches such as CCT and NT to address any irrational thoughts that may hinder biblical thinking. The PPC method promotes Christian intrapersonal formation and helps believers reduce cognitive conflict.

Unlike traditional pastoral counseling, which is typically reactive, PPC seeks to address intrapersonal conflict in individuals before it escalates. PPC encourages believers to revisit and reframe their internal struggles by enhancing biblical literacy and promoting daily spiritual disciplines. Like pastoral counseling, PPC fosters a Christlike atmosphere and provides a safe space where individuals can share their hearts openly and without fear of judgment. By cultivating trust through the counselor-client relationship and group interactions, PPC facilitates intrapersonal and interpersonal communication, enabling participants to understand themselves and others better. This approach leads to Christian intrapersonal formation, reduces inner conflict, and empowers believers to walk in the ways of Christ confidently.

— 4 —

The Efficacy of PPC Among Believers

OVER SIX WEEKS, THE six members at *Church S* voluntarily submitted to the CIF training course implemented by *Proactive* Pastoral Counseling, a Christlike CIT. A Christian environment set the stage for each week's *proactive* pastoral counseling sessions. This chapter discusses the nature of each week and those results.

In the first week, a comprehensive assessment tool was employed to evaluate each member before the program commenced. Over the following five weeks, the sessions delved into the intrapersonal struggles stemming from the identified problem and examined the impact on each believer. Each week's session focused on one of the five most prevalent church-related issues affecting the hearts and minds of the congregation at *Church S* (refer to weeks two through six). The outcomes of the four-step CIF process are detailed in the summary, encompassing both individual and collective group responses.

The Efficacy of PPC Among Believers

Overview

Proactive Pastoral Counseling seeks to help decrease intrapersonal conflict in others while developing Christian intrapersonal formation. Wilkins says, "Counseling from a Christian perspective covers a variety of problems for people: helping people deal with severe loss, conflict resolution, stress management or elimination, and other issues that plague individuals."[1] In this light, the CIF program succeeded on many levels.

Each week during the CIF program, participants' self-reflection in Christ grew (Eph 4:22–24). One might suggest a moral shift occurred within the group, and the awareness of one's spiritual ethics heightened. Leaf suggests, "A person's moral nature results from God impressing His moral standards on their soul."[2] Participants became more aware they were not alone in their struggle with faith at *Church S*.

Gathering in a Christian small group setting, participants began to develop trust within the group.[3] As each member lessened one's condemnation in the heart and became more confident (as in 1 John 3:21), internal struggles began surfacing, and participants started sharing them without fear of rejection or judgment—spiritual confidence increased individually and as a group. Interestingly, participants learned truthful insights into why people felt like they did about their church-related issue(s).

The essence of the CIF training program began taking shape in steps 2 and 3 of the program. Whereas step 1 addressed the nature of the problem, steps 2 and 3 encouraged the participant to seek God's Word for overall spiritual support. While referring to 2 Timothy 3:14–17, the pastoral counselor pointed out the importance of reading the Bible and understanding its underlying spiritual applications, especially when approaching each week's problem. As a result, participants learned to see their stories from a biblical perspective and not just from their own (Prov 3:5–6), and new insights about

---

1. Wilkins, "Educating the Congregation," 51.
2. Leaf, "Maintaining a Biblical Worldview," 42.
3. Haugk, *Stephen Ministry*, 15.

their life narratives (past and present) and future spiritual goals began to take shape (as described in Luke 9:23).

Subsequently, the high-spirited approach from the pastoral counselor accentuated the small-group discussions—his pastoral presence and identity were evident. As more trust developed, group members opened up with each other, and a sense of synergy developed. Liu, Zhu, and Turner mention, "Group cohesiveness is a dynamic and bilateral process involving various intrapersonal and interpersonal processes."[4]

In step 4, participants began realizing their stories of woes, suffering, and complaints had value. Although step 4 addressed irrational thinking, each participant's struggle helped bring about the life struggle in others. As such, by listening to the testimonies of others, members gained new insights about the accuracy of their internal processes. Eubanks notes, "Maybe their internal guidance system isn't as broken as they feared."[5]

From one perspective, CIF guides individuals to steer away from secular thinking when addressing intrapersonal struggles. Each week's problem was examined through a biblical lens, helping participants realize that the counselor-client relationship is a spiritual discipline rather than just a therapy session. Promoting therapy as a spiritual discipline has the potential to motivate believers to seek profound personal and communal transformation.[6]

Although it took some time, participants noticed themselves shifting spiritually throughout the program—they began to see growth in each other. Essentially, CIF's biblical approach to coping with intrapersonal conflict spawned a "transformation of the mind" in believers (Rom 12:2). This new life suggests that when believers start paying attention to what goes into their minds, they can stop the cognitive cycle of disintegration and embrace the acts of confession and repentance that lead to redemption. In this, one

---

4. Liu et al., "Counselor Trainees' Personal Growth," 14.
5. Eubanks, *How We Relate*, 210.
6. White, "Conceptualizing Therapy," 97.

might better understand why Paul links regeneration with the healing, or integration, of the mind.[7]

Overall, the CIF training course emphasized how to approach internal issues better and those embedded in the *Church S* community. The CIF four-step training program supplied the tools others needed to cope better (Christian formation) with intrapersonal struggles, increase biblical literacy, and grow toward Christlikeness. As Harris notes, "Curriculums are valuable tools that have been used throughout history and are helpful in intentionally equipping others."[8] CIF also helped participants better understand how to manage ongoing personal struggles such as low self-esteem and self-worth and the fear of rejection. Each participant gained new spiritual truths about their lives while better understanding the reason behind their intrapersonal struggles.

At the end of the course, it was discovered that each participant achieved an elevated sense of awareness about their internal narratives. At the same time, by applying spiritual disciplines more intentionally, believers experienced a more profound, relational knowing of self and God, which is inherently transformational. As a result, what emerges is the best version of ourselves, held in deep intimacy with the Triune God.[9] Each believer envisioned their life and struggles with a new hope (1 Pet 1:3–6). The participants left the CIF training program feeling more biblically literate, less conflicted internally, and inspired with a new confidence in their walk with Christ.

Demographic Backgrounds

The demographic information of each member is intended only to describe the general nature of each group member. Age, gender, vocation, marital status, family life, personal struggles, intrapersonal management skills, and personal characteristics ranging

---

7. Thompson, *Anatomy of the Soul*, 184.
8. Harris, "Christocentric Discipleship," 81.
9. White, "Conceptualizing Therapy," 93.

from early childhood to adulthood are mentioned. Although some discussion on drug and alcohol abuse was had, it was ascertained not to be a component of the course as no participant struggled with those addictions in the past or at the time of participating in the CIF training program.

Participant #1 (P1): Steve

Steve (P1) is a sixty-four-year-old Caucasian male raised on a farm by his parents in Honesdale, PA. After his high school graduation, P1 earned a certificate in auto mechanics at college, later working as a propane truck driver and in "receiving" at a paper mill. Steve has been married twice, has two children, and describes himself as a loner, shy, sensitive to others, and a "momma's boy."

Growing up on the farm, Steve struggled with making healthy connections and was often bullied by his peers. Similarly, when asked about his relationship with his father, P1 responded, "My dad was a tough guy, and his discipline was rough." As a result, P1 never learned how to manage his emotions and developed anger as a way to cope with his struggles.

Steve's childhood "bully" struggles permeated into his married life. He began feeling adverse opposition from his wife, noting, "She was always against me." After reaching a point of irreconcilability in the relationship, they divorced, and Steve began to struggle with depression and anxiety. After voluntarily seeking professional care, Steve was diagnosed with Chronic Depressive Disorder (CDD)[10] and now (after twenty-five years) manages his condition with assorted medications. Steve is now retired and disabled from multiple health issues but serves faithfully as an usher and greeter at *Church S*.

---

10. With this condition, one suffers from continuous episodes of sadness, emptiness, and the lack of motivation. Low self-esteem and feelings of worthlessness and hopelessness are common. Mayo Clinic, "Persistent Depressive Disorder."

Participant #2 (P2): Clarice

Clarice (P2) is a sixty-seven-year-old Caucasian female raised by her parents in Brooklyn, NY. Clarice attended a Catholic school for girls as a youth and later graduated from high school there. At twenty-one, Clarice married and began working as a secretary at an insurance firm—she later became a "stay-at-home mom," raising her two boys. While at home, P2 earned an associate degree in nursing. Clarice later became an adult caregiver, working in multiple genres of caregiving (nursing, geriatrics, CNA) throughout her career.

Growing up in Brooklyn, Clarice struggled with making friends and maintaining healthy relationships. When asked about her family togetherness, she said, "I became defiant early on because my parents never let me do anything." In her rebellion, P2 turned to herself for guidance and purposely inhibited others from connecting with her inwardly (including her parents). P2's inability to cope produced irrational thinking—"I will never meet my parents' expectations"—using blame as a defense mechanism to protect herself from present or future hurt. P2 became distant from others, never learning how to build healthy relationships.

As a result, Clarice struggled with self-judgment, low self-esteem, and the inability to connect with others. Having no luck with self-help books to deal with her intrapersonal conflict, P2 sought help from a psychiatrist but was unsuccessful. Eventually, P2 was hospitalized twice for Persistent Depressive Disorder[11] and now struggles with Seasonal Affective Disorder.[12] Although P2 has been taking medications for thirty-four years to manage her condition(s), Clarice maintains an active membership at *Church S* with her second husband, serving in church hospitality for nearly twenty years.

---

11. White, "Conceptualizing Therapy," 97.
12. Mayo Clinic, "Seasonal Affective Disorder."

Participant #3 (P3): Sara

Sara (P3), born in Louisville, KY, is a sixty-four-year-old Caucasian female raised by her mom in Harmony, ME. After graduating high school, P3 married and raised three children while staying home. Twenty-nine years later, her husband had an affair, and they separated. With no possibility of reconciling the relationship, they decided to separate permanently but stayed married for the children's sake. She describes herself as a quiet, shy, introverted, girly-girl, non-athletic, who loves reading.

Sara struggled throughout her marriage to overcome the void she experienced as a child from the divorce of her parents—she lost the relationship she once had with her father. Although her confidence needed work and she had few friends, Sara learned to adapt at home alone in private. In many cases, Sara confronted her issues (early on) using drugs and alcohol—no one was there to turn to for support. She still struggles with confidence issues but has learned how to manage her feelings of emptiness. Interestingly, Sara has no addictions, no medical or clinical conditions, and takes no medications.

Despite all her struggles, Sara maintains faithful involvement with *Church S*, serving within various ministries, such as hospitality and church administration. Sara has been a steadfast believer (Christian) for thirty-five years.

Participant #4 (P4): Jasper

Jasper (P4) is a thirty-year-old Native American male born and raised by his parents in Baltimore, MD. After graduating high school, P4 attended college but soon dropped out and was married, finding work as an electrician with his father. A few years later, he and his wife moved to New England, where they became the owner-operators of a small-town general store. P4 describes himself as obnoxious, loud, annoying, abrasive, hardworking, and kind-hearted, and at times exhibits behavior like that of a comedian.

Jasper's greatest family struggle was maintaining a healthy relationship with his mother. From early on, P4 sought a connection with his mother but was restricted due to his fear of her and how she might react to him. As a result, P4 struggles with reaching out to others, which he recognizes stems from his inability to cope with inner conflict. His philosophy of coping: "I just ignore it." Jasper also struggles with anger, depression, anxiety, and self-hate issues.

Similarly, P4 struggles with low self-esteem and an inability to confront internal conflict. Although P4 is not taking any medications currently, he was diagnosed with ADHD as a youth (third through eighth grades). He had, in the past, also been prescribed a marijuana card to manage his anger, depression, and anxiety. Regardless of his past issues, P4 is now an active member at *Church S* and serves as an associate pastor (youth pastor). P4 has been a believer for fourteen years and strives to grow his business in rural New England.

Participant #5 (P5): Kelly

Kelly (P5) is a thirty-one-year-old Caucasian female born and raised by her mom in Baltimore, MD. After graduating high school, P5 began her educational advancement and attended college for nursing, where she eventually met her future husband and was married. After earning her RN status and working in the NICU for five years, P5 moved to New England and became the owner of a small-town convenience store. She describes herself as kind, compassionate, emotional, intelligent, empathetic, and hardworking.

As a child, Kelly struggled emotionally, first with the loss of her father and then with bullying. P5 developed trust issues, closed herself off from others, and withdrew from those around her, making it hard to make friends. Without a therapeutic option to help her, P5 dove inwardly to cope with her conflict. P5 is still greatly affected by her past and struggles even more now since her mom has passed. Although she is taking no medications at this time, P5 has been diagnosed with anxiety and depression and has been on and off prescription medications for ten years.

P5 exhibits compassionate care toward others daily. P5 has served in multiple ministry settings, such as helping people without transportation, kids' ministries, and providing moral support to those in need. P5 has been a believer (Christian) for twenty years and continues working as a nurse where there is a need.

Participant #6 (P6): Edith

Edith (P6) is a sixty-five-year-old Caucasian female born and raised by her parents in Springfield, MA. After graduating high school, P6 married but got a divorce after thirteen years, keeping her two children with her. In that process, Edith realized she wanted to be a caregiver, and at thirty-five, she began her caregiving career working with adults with disabilities. Twenty-five years later, P6 left her job due to COVID-19 but remains available for private care when needed. P6 describes herself as witty, funny, generous to a fault, struggling with trust issues, loyal to friends and family, and selfless.

As a youth, P6 struggled deeply due to the limited ability she had to spend time with her dad (work-related). She was also unable to connect with her mother and was bullied at school. As a result, she developed trust issues, withdrew from others, and became dependent upon her grandmother to help her manage the struggles she endured with her mom and life. When asked, "How do you cope with the struggles that come into your life?" she said, "Anything I am not able to deal with, I don't think or speak about. I bury it." P6 has been diagnosed with depression and anxiety and currently takes medications for her condition(s).

Despite her struggles with trust, P6 actively supports her community by volunteering at the local food bank and providing caregiving services (cooking, cleaning, ministry of presence) to people who need physical care (stroke victims, disabled). P6 manages her intrapersonal conflict by making home quilts, crocheting, and embroidery. Edith is a believer (Christian) of fifty-six years and lives as a widow with her friends and family in New England.

Data Analysis

For six weeks, *Proactive* Pastoral Counseling implemented its Christian Intrapersonal Formation training course for six actively involved Christian believers. In those sessions, five of the most prevalent problems experienced at *Church S* were discussed, evaluated, and analyzed through each participant's personal testimonies and life narratives. As Sensing states, "The participants in the project are often the most valuable sources of evaluation for your project. . . . Your expertise as the minister, researcher, and active participant will be the filter of all the data."[13]

The results of the CIF program emphasize PPC is possible for those (Christians and non-Christians) willing to submit to Christian intrapersonal formation. Incidentally, PPC and the CIF training programs are not exclusive to *Church S* but intend to reach other congregations and communities. With that in mind, *Church S* agreed to participate in the CIF training program, encompassing a case-study approach using a blended tool to measure Christian intrapersonal formation. The following section details the combined results of employing those tools.

Initial Assessment: One-on-One Interview

Each participant was asked the following five questions in a one-on-one interview in week one of class:

1. How would you describe your walk with Christ?
2. How often during the week do you submit to spiritual disciplines, such as reading the Bible and prayer?
3. How do you feel about the "You" in you right now?
4. Why have you chosen to participate in the CIF training program?
5. What do you seek to learn from the CIF training course?

---

13. Sensing, *Qualitative Research*, 151.

Answers provided by each participant varied and were based on the nature of each question.

For example, question one asks the participant to define their present relationship status with Christ. In this case, responses were recorded using three categories: "Close," "Okay," or "Needs Work." Question two asks how often spiritual disciplines are practiced weekly, noted by 1–3/week, 4–6/week, or every day. Question three is specific to how one might feel toward oneself, such as "I Feel Good About Me," "Needs Work," "Bad About Me," or "I Don't Know." Stokes says, "A Christian counselor could assert a Christian accommodative treatment like intradisciplinary integration as useful for effecting outcomes that are good psychologically but are even better spiritually for Christian counselees."[14]

Question four narrows down the individuals' purpose for taking the class, categorizing their responses as "Increase Self-Awareness," "Strengthen Coping Skills," or "Grow in Christ." Finally, question five provides three categories to determine what each individual seeks to accomplish by undergoing the CIF training program: decrease intrapersonal struggles, increase biblical literacy, and grow in Christlikeness. Figure 1 below represents each participant's response to one of the five one-on-one interview questions.

Fig. 1. Initial Interview

Question One:	Close	OK	Needs Work
Steve	X		
Clarice		X	
Sara	X		
Jasper			X
Kelly			X
Edith			X

14. Stokes, "Heart, Soul, Mind, and Strength," 40.

Initial Assessment: Feelings Vocabulary List

Following the one-on-one interview, a feelings vocabulary list was provided for each participant to select words that might evaluate their emotional well-being and represent their present feeling. In other words, each participant was asked to pick a word that best described their emotional state at the beginning and end of class. Comparatively, an emotion graph is provided each week to display the shift of emotion each participant experienced while taking the CIF course. Figure 2 below provides an example.

Fig. 2. Week One Individual Emotions

Participant Feeling:	Beginning of Class	End of Class
Steve	Achy	Unfocused
Clarice	Impatient	Relaxed
Sara	Interested	Excited
Jasper	Anxious	Motivated
Kelly	Tired	Happy
Edith	Curious	Uplifted

Initial Assessment: Spiritual Evaluation

The initial spiritual evaluation worksheet provided by the counselor assessed the understanding of theological concepts and themes, biblical terminology awareness, and how one might define one's relationship with Christ. Some suggest there is a benefit for counselor educators to outline mechanisms that might procure personal growth.[15] Spiritual aptitude was measured by word choice per letter prompt and the ability to fill in all letter prompts.

For example, one might choose "Christian" as the word choice for the letter C prompt (C—Christian). However, the word "crucified" would be a "best fit" (C—Crucified) scenario as it focuses more on Christ and not the individual. In some cases, more than

---

15. Liu et al., "Counselor Trainees' Personal Growth," 25–26.

one word was a best-fit solution (S—Sacrifice, Salvation, Servant). As an example, the "A" prompt was provided for each participant (Atonement). A best-fit solution was noted in parentheses.

Four Marks of a Disciple Questionnaire

The biblical persona of each participant was measured by examining four marks of a biblical disciple. The questionnaire produced each participant's understanding of how they might compare to a biblical disciple. The four marks included Servant, Evangelist, Worshiper, and Missionary.

Per each mark, participants assessed seven statements, comparing themselves by choosing a rating of one to five. Figure 3 below gives a display of what that looks like.

Fig. 3. Missionary Mark

MISSIONARY	Strongly Disagree	Disagree	Neither Agree nor Disagree	Agree	Strongly Agree
	1	2	3	4	5
I believe in the work of missions					
I accept people for who they are					
I think of others more than myself					
I love to engage with others for Christ					
I enjoy sharing my life with others					
Living in a different country has always appealed to me					
Living for Jesus is my lifestyle, not a routine					
SUMMARY OF MARKS					
TOTAL POINT					

The Efficacy of PPC Among Believers

Upon completion, a tally was taken using a Likert scale (thirty-five points possible per category), with each participant's highest and lowest marks being recorded. A high score indicated the mark most closely related to the participant, whereas a low score represented the least in comparison. As an example, see Figure 4.

Fig. 4. Four Marks of a Disciple Questionnaire

Four Marks of a Disciple:	Servant	Evangelist	Worshiper	Missionary
Steve			X—High	X—Low
Clarice			X—High	X—Low
Sara		X—Low	X—High	
Jasper	X—Low			X—High
Kelly			X—High	X—Low
Edith	X—High			X—Low

CIF Program: Weeks Two Through Six

In week one, the CIF small group selected the five most pressing issues affecting their faith and spiritual well-being at *Church S*. Each group member expressed the problem and why it should be addressed. In weeks two through six, those problems were approached by implementing PPC and the CIF four-step program.

First, the week's problem was defined, intrapersonal struggles were examined, and the effect of those struggles was noted. Second, Scripture was sought for study to understand how to combat the issue. Third, once Scripture had been reviewed, the pastoral counselor helped each individual better understand the content and its spiritual applications for administering to the problem. Fourth, therapeutic approaches such as CCT, CBT, and NT were used to identify psychological inhibitors (triggers) that might keep one from thinking biblically.

In so doing, each week's sessions produced a high volume of responses. Each specific response was recorded, analyzed, and tallied collectively, composing a "group response." The group response, then, is the accumulation of the most commonly stated reactions from each individual in the group. Data collected stemmed from various questions, such as, "What is the problem?" "Why is the problem a problem for the participant?" "What is the intrapersonal struggle most associated with the problem?" "How does the intrapersonal struggle affect each participant?"

In the same way, in steps two and three, each participant responded biblically to the problem. The responses were tallied and analyzed, producing a group response outlining the PPC approach and how CIF manifests. In contrast, step 4 identifies adverse thinking that might inhibit one from applying biblical thinking and displays the responses from a group perspective. The participants' feelings are shown to highlight any change of emotion that might have occurred throughout each class.

Week Two: Problem #1—Lack of Spiritual Leadership

Problem 1 looked at *Church S*'s "Lack of Spiritual Leadership." Men at *Church S* who were given ecclesiastical authority failed to lead the congregation spiritually. Jasper mentioned, "The men are more focused on the rules than growing in Christ." Kelly and Clarice felt unfairly treated, stating, "I did not belong in the church clique." Edith experienced trust issues with other members, bringing back negative memories from her past experiences with other churches. Ultimately, the group was not learning spiritual things because the men who led *Church S* were religion-minded instead of Spirit-filled.[16]

The group felt neglected, lacking unity, distant, and disconnected from others, deflating any personal desire to serve others. Essentially, the desire to be fed spiritually led to disappointment. They also struggled with internal notions such as, "No one cares about me," "Why go to church if my needs are not being met?" and more specifically, "What is wrong with me?" Sara was frustrated

---

16. Marshall and Newheiser, *When Words Matter*, 40.

and often unable to cope with apathetic people and became quite frustrated.

Furthermore, Steve and Clarice experienced an increase in their depression. Like Jasper and Kelly, they stopped attending church weekly, feeling unworthy of participating in the services. Sara felt alone in her walk with Christ and developed negative coping skills toward others. Edith lost trust in others and felt unequipped to build new relationships. The group suffered from decreased spiritual growth and fought to maintain their Christian walk.

However, the group's thinking renewed when viewing the problem from a biblical perspective. Clarice recognized her life focus was in the wrong place and refocused her spiritual motivations (Luke 9:23). Steve experienced a decrease in his depression by casting all his cares on the Lord (1 Pet 5:7). Jasper and Kelly recognized the same as Sara, noting permanent resolve to intrapersonal struggle is to turn to God for understanding (Prov 3:5–6). Edith proclaimed, "God is my refuge, not man" (Ps 118:8) and became enlightened (see figure 5 for individual emotions).

Fig. 5. Week Two Individual Emotions

Participant Feeling:	Beginning of Class	End of Class
Steve	Restless	Focused
Clarice	Refreshed	Sad
Sara	Curious	Interested
Jasper	Eager	Determined
Kelly	Tired	Lifted
Edith	Exhausted	Worthy

Week Three: Problem #2—Spiritual Apathy

Week three discussed "Spiritual Apathy," wherein participants viewed *Church S* as lacking interest, enthusiasm, or concern over spiritual growth and Christian outreach. Steve and Jasper acknowledged people's behavior as a social activity, stating, "They are all just going through the motions: no one cares!" Clarice described the church as having "no life. There was no real sense of fellowship." Sara mentioned, "No one is ministry-minded. There is no love of the Spirit. No one is sensitive to His leading." Kelly and Edith refrained from serving altogether, fearing that asking others for ministry help might produce personal rejection. In short, no one wanted to do anything spiritual.

Spiritual apathy at *Church S* left all the participants feeling divided, unsatisfied, and distant. Although the group's desire for ministry and fellowship was great, they struggled with the lack of interest in others to build spiritual relationships. The group noted, "Fellowship at *Church S* seems to extend only to a monthly potluck." Sara asked, "Where is Christ?"

Some told themselves they were the problem. Others felt unworthy of themselves or not good enough, and anxiety and depression increased. Some group members no longer desired to attend *Church S*, even after years of attendance. They felt rejected, struggled with Christian friendships, and found no one interested in ministry work. The church was disconnected, and those spiritually discerning were set aside.

Fig. 6. Week Three Individual Emotions

Participant Feeling:	Beginning of Class	End of Class
Steve	Peaceful	Excellent
Clarice	Serene	Refreshed
Sara	Relaxed	Content
Jasper	Anxious	Motivated
Kelly	Interested	Relaxed
Edith	Confident	Worthy

Addressing the situation biblically, the minds of each participant realized an approach that had not yet been taken. The group recognized that they were all thinking in the flesh, not the Spirit. Steve suggested focusing on living in the Spirit (Gal 5:16–18). Jasper commented, "If your mind is on the flesh, then you have no interest in doing things for the Spirit" (Rom 8:5). Edith mentioned, "People who are apathetic spiritually will not listen to God's Word." The group acknowledged that staying focused on God's Word helps guard their mind from dwelling on the failures of others. They were all moved (see figure 6 for individual emotions).

Week Four: Problem #3—Lack of Faith

The book of Hebrews states, "Faith is the assurance of things hoped for, the conviction of things not seen" (Heb 11:1). *Church S* struggles greatly with practicing faith in that they place their trust not in God but in themselves. In other words, *Church S* submits to religious motivations compelled by self-preservation, holding firmly to a preference-driven church.[17] Steve commented, "My walk with Christ started to suffer."

The greatest struggle the group experienced manifested in the desire to be taught how to have more faith in their lives. Unfortunately, the heart of the church centered its worship around self-pursuits instead of being other-focused, so building faith in others was not a concept for *Church S*. The CIF small group noticed questioning their faith increased, and their spiritual growth became stunted. As such, Sara asked, "How can I grow in faith if faith is not something on the table to eat?"

Additionally, adverse thinking among the group increased. Steve felt *Church S* tried to manipulate him, making him think he was wrong about the whole faith idea—tried telling him something other than the truth. Some of the group thought they were the problem in that they needed to know more about biblical things. Others questioned, "Why am I here?" whereas others expressed that they were the cause of the problem. Ultimately, they were confused about faith and did not have anyone to help them understand how to manage faith issues.

Turning to Scripture, participants began to see the struggle with faith they had been experiencing all along was the very thing

---

17. Rainer, *Autopsy of a Deceased Church*, 29.

that was helping them grow in faith (Acts 20:22). In that, the group realized others who are supposed to demonstrate faith might not even have faith themselves. They noted, "One can know Jesus but never come into faith with Him. In short, if no one teaches faith, they don't have it."

The CIF process helped remind the group that faith comes from hearing God's Word (Rom 10:17). Kelly said, "Right! Although someone else might not have faith or teach how to have faith, we grow by seeking God, not man." Sara exclaimed, "I get it now! Fight the faithless with faith" (Eph 6:10–17).

Week Five: Problem #4—Spiritual Oppression

The CIF small group defined spiritual oppression as "an outside force being forced upon another person." They understood feelings of being oppressed associated with being weighed down spiritually, overburdened emotionally, and having a constant feeling of being controlled. In other words, spiritual oppression is what happens when people grow their own sense of power, comfort, and security at the expense of others. Steve described spiritual oppression as "constant satanic attacks on the mind."

While discussing the problem, Jasper commented, "Spiritual oppression is damaging. It is the worst of kinds, and some people never get over being hurt by those who call themselves Christians." The group responded, "I feel I am always in a spiritual fight, with myself, for myself." Clarice said, "It is hard to get up emotionally when constantly beaten spiritually. My depression already takes hold of me enough." Some believed they would never be good enough, stating, "How can I be approved if they are always oppressing me?" The group realized they were stuck in themselves, "living in the *Church S* void."

The group grew in frustration daily, depression and anxiety heightened, and they withdrew from other members of *Church S*. Not only that, participants stopped reading their Bibles, failed to attend church faithfully, and looked elsewhere for spiritual help. Spiritual decline progressed, and the group suffered in their thinking. Fighting adverse cognition, the group slowly began changing their inner dialogues, saying, "I'm not adequate, not worthy enough for this place. I am not equipped to deal with this kind of spiritual warfare."

Turning to Scripture helped bring the group's thinking "out of the *Church S* void." They recognized they had turned to themselves for help as though they were losing spiritual strength. After a review of Scripture, Clarice noted the power of God in her, saying, "The Lord will renew my strength" (Isa 40:31). Edith realized after all her years in church what "He is my Rock and stronghold" meant (Ps 62:1–2).

Overall, the group was strengthened, spiritually. They were reminded that strength for the battle comes from the power only God gives. Realizing that power comes by standing firm on God's Word, the group responded, "Placing God's Word in your mind while on the battlefield gives you the strength to fight against the forces of spiritual oppression. Let's try that!" (2 Cor 10:4–5; see figure 7 for individual emotions).

Fig. 7. Week Five Individual Emotions

Participant Feeling:	Beginning of Class	End of Class
Steve	Excited	Energized
Clarice	Rattled	Hopeful
Sara	Disappointed	Regretful
Jasper	Worried	Encouraged
Kelly	Displaced	Interested
Edith	Hopeful	Calm

Week Six: Problem #5—Inability to Communicate

The inability to communicate within *Church S*'s walls holds many perspectives. The CIF small group agrees that the failure to communicate is possibly the most spiritually damaging of all the problems discussed in the past six weeks. Specifically, members of

Church S neglect or refuse face-to-face conversations with ministry-minded individuals—the "New England" way is not spiritual. Nonetheless, the lack of communication is not that communication at *Church S* does not exist; it exists to create stories between others that do not exist, creating false truth narratives that destroy the good character of others (see Neh 6:1–8).

In that light, *Church S* members "take offense" when confronted with accountability issues and back-talk those holding them spiritually accountable. In other words, they spread gossip to shame and defame those holding them spiritually responsible, reflecting the nature of people in 1 Timothy 4:1–2.

In perspective, the CIF group agreed that the communication problem at *Church S* is spiritual but stems from Puritan roots—a religiously enhanced, culturally generated curse.[18] The following is a range of viewpoints the CIF small group compiled while grappling with their personal challenges related to the "inability to communicate" issue at *Church S*:

- *Church S* avoids direct communication with others because they fear being exposed as non-Christians.

- At *Church S*, discussing spiritual matters exceeds their biblical comprehension. Since they lack an understanding of spiritual concepts, they cannot engage in meaningful conversations with spiritually inclined people. Instead, they resort to gossiping behind people's backs, as it is their chosen means of communication.

- *Church S* dismisses anything they do not want to hear, even if it is grounded in the Bible, insisting, "They want what they want."

- If something does not matter to *Church S*, it holds no significance. This sense of devaluation for others may explain why there is no ministry at *Church S*, as ministry necessitates genuine interpersonal communication and concern for others, not gossip and spiritual indifference.

18. Pilsbury and Allen, *History of Methodism*, 5.

The Efficacy of PPC Among Believers

- *Church S* is apprehensive about evangelism because they are unsure of what to say; their focus is on religious formalities rather than a genuine spiritual mindset.

- *Church S* grapples with communication hurdles due to a lack of guidance on engaging with outsiders; a cultural barrier shields them by distancing individuals before forming connections. Curiously, this deficiency in communication skills might also signify a difficulty in grasping spiritual matters; *progression often demands learning.*

- *Church S* members prioritize self-preservation, showing little concern for others. The prevailing sentiment, echoing the slogan of *Church S*, is "If you're not from New England, you're 'From Away.' If you're 'from away,' you're not part of us, even if you are the pastor. We are in charge, not God!" In short, Christians and the work of the Holy Spirit threaten the religious structure and control of *Church S* over its members *and* community.

- *Church S* refuses to change, and anyone who brings change is ostracized, particularly Christians. Christians are persecuted, shunned, and forced out of town. *Church S* refuses to accept the truth and slanders anyone in the name of Christ. They do not want to believe the truth, for they will be exposed to their evil deeds and be forced to lose control of themselves and the members of the church.

Similarly, the group observed that individuals native to New England communicate differently than those from other regions. For example, "Go around the barn" describes circulating a story behind someone's back, with different versions debated until a consensus is reached. This practice resembles a collective mentality, almost like a mob, where the goal is to get everyone, except outsiders, to agree on a narrative and accept it as truth.

Unfortunately, this approach encourages deception and the spread of gossip and falsehoods, which people often believe (as highlighted in the "Pass the Phrase" exercise during week one). As a result, the truth becomes obscured, and those who stand for it (more often than not) experience behavior unbecoming of a Christian. Sara remarked, "Perhaps this is why direct communication is avoided: People do not speak what they truly feel for fear of being ostracized. Instead, they gossip."

Because gossip supersedes the truth at *Church S*, fellowship between members sometimes causes a significant rift, causing a broader disconnect that produces more gossip. Kelly expressed, "They are not true. People put on fake smiles, but deep down inside, they mean something else. I feel unwelcome." As with Edith, trusting others became an everyday issue. She said, "I no longer wanted to communicate for fear of how others might twist what I say, then turn it around as something I never said to put me down while making themselves look better."

Overall, participants became stressed, mad, anxious, and felt alone. The group often took matters into their own hands for their own protection. Although they struggled with thinking ill of others, they desired to connect deep down.

For Clarice and Steve, they struggled with their depression so much that they stopped attending regularly. Many in the group stopped reading their Bibles. The entire CIF group noted, "It affected me personally and deeply. I wanted to retaliate with harm." Jasper, Kelly, and Edith said, "I am not biblically literate to handle this as a Christian." Some thought, "Maybe I am what they say about me, even though they did not say it to me directly."

The inability to communicate also created negative motivations with other members. Sara felt compelled to address everyone's wrongs daily. Steve wanted to shoot the windows out at the church. Clarice lost herself and wanted nothing to do with any of them. Edith fought with her trust issues, and Kelly struggled to overcome her emotions. The problem with the inability to communicate created an inability for others to see the truth, and each participant struggled immensely.

However, when turning to Scripture, the life in each participant was stirred. Steve notes, "You can walk through the talk when you have the talk (God's Words) to walk" (as in Luke 10:19). Jasper was encouraged by his study of James 1:19, which impresses, "Be quick to hear, and slow to speak." Edith found new Scripture and application: "I never thought to just dwell on God's Word, or consider it honorable, pure, and lovely. It changes things for me" (as in Phil 4:8). The problem with the lack of communication affected everyone deeply. Still, they became empowered by God's Word and moved forward (see figure 8 for individual emotions).

Fig. 8. Week Six Individual Emotions

Participant Feeling:	Beginning of Class	End of Class
Steve	Frustrated	Fantastic
Clarice	Content	Content
Sara	Lively	Joyful
Jasper	Exhausted	Encouraged
Kelly	Stressed	Lifted
Edith	Inspired	Worthy

Final Assessment: One-on-One Interview

At the end of the CIF training class, each participant was asked five follow-up questions in a one-on-one interview to measure growth (if any) from the initial interview in week one. They are as follows:

1. Since your initial interview, how has your relationship with Christ changed?
2. What spiritual disciplines have become steadier in your life because of CIF?
3. How do you feel about the "You" in you right now?
4. What new insights or personal awareness have you experienced from participating in the CIF training program?
5. How has CIF helped you grow toward Christlikeness?

Answers provided by each participant varied and were based on the nature of each question (see figure 9 for an example).

Fig. 9. Final Interview

Question One:	Significantly	Some Change	Not So Much
Steve	X		
Clarice	X		
Sara	X		
Jasper	X		
Kelly		X	
Edith	X		

Final Assessment: Spiritual Evaluation

The initial spiritual evaluation worksheet provided by the counselor assessed the understanding of theological concepts and themes, biblical terminology awareness, and how one might define one's relationship with Christ. The final assessment provides the same worksheet to assess changes in one's ability to evaluate things from a biblical perspective. The worksheet was given to each participant at the end of the CIF training course. The results are defined more clearly in the next section.

Summary of Results

This portion of chapter 4 provides an overall tally of responses from the participants who submitted to the CIF program. The *proactive* pastoral counselor used a blended tool and weekly journal entries from class discussions to measure Christian intrapersonal formation. The following final assessments summarize the findings procured by the CIF training course.

Four Marks of a Disciple

The Four Marks of a Disciple questionnaire was used to define the view of each participant when compared to the traits of a biblical disciple. Four marks were used: Servant, Evangelist, Worshiper, and Missionary. However, there is no right or wrong answer; the tool depicts how each individual perceives themselves compared to a biblical perspective. High scoring represents the most closely related, whereas low scoring represents the most unrelated to each mark. An overall tally was performed to note the high and low marks collectively within the group.

For example, four participants related most to the worshiper mark, four were most unrelated to the missionary mark, and one participant related most to a missionary. One participant noted themselves relating most to a servant and one was most unrelated to it. Edith was the only servant in the group, and evangelism was unrelated to most.

As such, 67 percent of the CIF group identified as worshipers, 67 percent identified themselves as unrelated to the mark of a missionary, and there were no evangelists. The group admits they lack servanthood and evangelistic pursuits but agrees their spiritual motivations are reflected in their heart for worship (see figure 10).

Fig. 10. Four Marks of a Disciple Questionnaire

Four Marks of a Disciple:	Servant	Evangelist	Worshiper	Missionary
Steve			X—High	X—Low
Clarice			X—High	X—Low
Sara		X—Low	X—High	
Jasper	X—Low			X—High
Kelly			X—High	X—Low
Edith	X—High			X—Low

Feelings Vocabulary List

Each week, participants were provided a vocabulary list of feelings to help them identify their emotions. The list of feelings was designed for participants to recognize, label, and record them to help identify any emotional changes resulting from the class. Similarly, the list's purpose was to help participants understand better how personal emotions surface, what triggers their feelings, and how to approach them without judgment. Changes in feelings help others identify any new nature that might arise among the participants.

Timoney suggests thoughts, feelings, and behaviors represent the newness of one's nature: they are the controlling factor.[19] Although all participants naturally experienced a change of feelings during class each week, lists of feelings for weeks one and six will be used to demonstrate the emotional shift in each individual and the group (see figure 12 below).

In week one, most participants felt anxious, impatient, and tired, whereas others in the CIF group expressed curiosity and interest in the class. Throughout the CIF program, participants' feelings ranged from being sad, agitated, exhausted, anxious, displaced, and worried about life, whereas other times, participants felt hopeful, confident, relaxed, and eager to learn more. At the end of class in week six, a final list of feelings was recorded and compared to each participant's feelings in week one (see figure 11).

Fig. 11. Final Assessment of Feelings

Participant Feeling:	Week One	Week Six
Steve	Achy	Fantastic
Clarice	Impatient	Content
Sara	Interested	Joyful
Jasper	Anxious	Encouraged
Kelly	Tired	Lifted
Edith	Curious	Worthy

Given this, each participant experienced an overall sense of well-being. By increasing one's biblical literacy and strengthening one's coping mechanisms with biblical terms and concepts, each participant's feelings changed for the better. Therefore, from a "feelings" perspective, Christian intrapersonal formation occurred

19. Timoney, "Identifying the Core Components," 11.

in one hundred percent of individuals who submitted to take the CIF training program.

Spiritual Assessment

The initial spiritual evaluation worksheet provided by the counselor assessed the understanding of theological concepts and themes, biblical terminology awareness, and how one might define one's relationship with Christ. The final spiritual assessment uses the same worksheet to compare changes within those parameters—any positive change represents Christian intrapersonal formation.

Spiritual aptitude was measured by two standards: the nature of the selected word per letter prompt and the individual's ability to fill in all letter prompts. CIF in everyone was evaluated by completion rate, the accuracy of word selection, and the number of times a "best-fit" word was used. On some level, CIF was experienced by each participant during this assessment.

For example, Steve completed the initial assessment with a 64 percent completion rate, whereas his completion rate was 100 percent in week six. Steve's initial accuracy rate was 60 percent, whereas his accuracy rate rose to 76 percent in week six. He also selected six best-fit words initially and seven best-fit words in the final assessment. Steve's completion rate increased by 36 percent, his accuracy rate improved by 16 percent, and his best-fit word choice increased by one (see figure 12).

Fig. 12. Steve's Spiritual Assessment

Steve	Initial Assessment	Final Assessment	+/-
Completion Rate	64% complete	100%	+36%
Accuracy of Word Selection	60% accurate	76%	+16%
Best-Fit Word	6	7	+1

Clarice completed the initial assessment with an 88 percent completion rate, whereas her completion rate was 100 percent in week six. Her initial accuracy rate was 52 percent, whereas her accuracy rate rose to 80 percent in week six. Clarice also selected five best-fit words initially and thirteen best-fit words in the final assessment. Clarice's completion rate increased by 12 percent, her accuracy rate improved by 28 percent, and her best-fit word choice increased by eight (see figure 13).

Fig. 13. Clarice's Spiritual Assessment

Clarice	Initial Assessment	Final Assessment	+/-
Completion Rate	88% complete	100%	+12%
Accuracy of Word Selection	52% accurate	80%	+28%
Best-Fit Word	5	13	+8

Sara completed the initial assessment with an 84 percent completion rate, whereas her completion rate was 100 percent in week six. Her initial accuracy rate was 60 percent, whereas her accuracy rate rose to 76 percent in week six. Sara also selected six best-fit words initially and eleven best-fit words in the final assessment. Sara's completion rate increased by 16 percent, her accuracy rate improved by 16 percent, and her best-fit word choice increased by five (see figure 14).

Fig. 14. Sara's Spiritual Assessment

Sara	Initial Assessment	Final Assessment	+/-
Completion Rate	84% complete	100%	+16%
Accuracy of Word Selection	60% accurate	76%	+16%
Best-Fit Word	6	11	+5

The Efficacy of PPC Among Believers

Jasper completed the initial assessment with an 88 percent completion rate, whereas his completion rate was 100 percent in week six. Jasper's initial accuracy rate was 60 percent, whereas his accuracy rate rose to 96 percent in week six. He also selected five best-fit words initially and seven best-fit words in the final assessment. Jasper's completion rate increased by 8 percent, his accuracy rate improved by 20 percent, and his best-fit word choice increased by two (see figure 15).

Fig. 15. Jasper's Spiritual Assessment

Jasper	Initial Assessment	Final Assessment	+/-
Completion Rate	88% complete	100%	+12%
Accuracy of Word Selection	60% accurate	96%	+36%
Best-Fit Word	5	7	+2

Kelly completed the initial assessment with a 44 percent completion rate, whereas her completion rate was 88 percent in week six. Her initial accuracy rate was 32 percent, whereas her accuracy rate rose to 64 percent in week six. Kelly also selected two best-fit words initially and five best-fit words in the final assessment, leaving her with seven best-fit words overall. Kelly's completion rate increased by 44 percent, her accuracy rate improved by 32 percent, and her best-fit word choice increased by three (see figure 16).

Fig. 16. Kelly's Spiritual Assessment

Kelly	Initial Assessment	Final Assessment	+/-
Completion Rate	44% complete	88%	+44%
Accuracy of Word Selection	32% accurate	64%	+32%
Best-Fit Word	2	5	+3

Edith completed the initial assessment with a 48 percent completion rate, whereas her completion rate was 88 percent in week six. Her initial accuracy rate was 64 percent, whereas her accuracy rate rose to 72 percent in week six. Edith also selected two best-fit words initially and seven best-fit words in the final assessment. Edith's completion rate increased by 40 percent, her accuracy rate improved by 8 percent, and her best-fit word choice increased by five (see figure 17).

Fig. 17. Edith's Spiritual Assessment

Edith	Initial Assessment	Final Assessment	+/-
Completion Rate	48% complete	88%	+40%
Accuracy of Word Selection	64% accurate	72%	+8%
Best-Fit Word	2	7	+5

Final Assessment: One-on-One Interview

One-on-one interviews are testimonies identifying where one might recognize oneself spiritually. Questions are formulated to elicit what the participant desires to learn, how they would like to grow, and what can be done to become more like Christ. At the end of the CIF training course, a final one-on-one interview with five questions was given and compared to the initial responses in week one. Each question in the final interview was related to the questions in week one, providing an opportunity to compose an overall comparison.

In question one, participants were asked to define their walk with Christ as "Good," "Okay," or "Needs Work." Initially, 16 percent felt good, 33 percent felt okay, and 50 percent felt their walk with Christ "needs work." The final interview asked if any change was made and to reflect that change by selecting "Significant," "Some Change," or "Not So Much." Comparatively, the results show that

The Efficacy of PPC Among Believers

100 percent of the CIF group experienced Christian intrapersonal formation, noting 83 percent expressed a significant change from week one, while 17 percent experienced some change. In short, all CIF group members grew closer in their relationship to Christ.

Question two asked about the use and frequency of spiritual disciplines in one's life. Bible reading, prayer, and journaling were three disciplines displayed. As a group, 50 percent of participants recognized an increase in their Bible reading, 33 percent maintained regular routines, whereas 16 percent began reading their Bible weekly. Some participants witnessed a 33 percent increase in their prayer life, whereas 83 percent experienced a deeper prayer life altogether.

Question three asked how the participants felt about their person. Initially, 50 percent showed a negative attitude toward themselves, whereas 50 percent of participants felt good about themselves. After implementing the CIF program, 100 percent of the group felt good about themselves, boosting overall morale by 50 percent. The final "feelings list" results also reflect a similar outcome (see figure 11).

Question four asked why the group member participated in the CIF training class. Three categories of measurement were provided: "Increase Self-Awareness," "Strengthen Coping Skills," and "Increase Christlikeness." Initially, 50 percent of participants took the class to increase their self-awareness, 16 percent desired to improve their coping skills, and 33 percent sought to grow in Christ. The results show each participant grew in Christian intrapersonal formation, 50 percent in self-awareness, 83 percent in strengthening coping skills, and 67 percent in growing one's relationship with Christ. Essentially, all participants significantly grew in all categories.

Question five asked the participants why they participated in the CIF training class. Three categories of measurement were also provided in this question: "Decrease Intrapersonal Conflict," "Increase Biblical Literacy," and "Increase Christlikeness." Initially, 50 percent of participants took the class to decrease intrapersonal conflict, 16 percent desired to increase biblical literacy, and 33 percent sought to grow in Christ. The results reveal that 100 percent of the class experienced CIF, increasing biblical literacy by 67 percent, decreasing intrapersonal conflict in 100 percent of the participants, and the group's relationship with Christ improved by 67 percent. Essentially, each participant grew significantly in all categories.

Counselor's Appraisal

Proactive Pastoral Counseling, a Christian Integrative Therapeutic, implemented its Christian Intrapersonal Formation training course for six active believers and was successful on all levels. Participants initially displayed curiosity and eagerness; yet, after learning how to manage one's world of feelings and emotions more appropriately, participants left the class feeling worthy and encouraged. Participants grew in the ability to assess life problems through increasing biblical literacy, leading to a decrease in intrapersonal conflict, an increase in self-awareness, and stronger coping skills while growing closer to Christ.

The CIF program worked exceptionally well for adult learners and young adults alike. It was interactive, personal, and enlightening, and everyone had an opportunity to learn more about themselves in a Christian light. Working the program in a small group forum, allowing participants to address their intrapersonal struggles, worked best to procure Christian intrapersonal formation. In contrast, the program did not experience significant difficulties or negative concerns.

Instead, Christian intrapersonal formation occurred in each individual in the CIF small group. The outline and approach of the CIF program was a great fit for meeting people right where they were, intrapersonally and interpersonally. As such, the counselor's notes intend to mention some things that worked, a few program challenges, and recommendations for future use.

First, providing a four-step approach to dealing with intrapersonal struggles helped participants better understand the importance of accurately (1) recognizing their issues, (2) accepting their problem with the problem at hand, (3) understanding the struggle and effect, and (4) learning how to manage those conflicts from a biblical perspective. In so doing, most participants began realizing that steps 1 through 4 of the CIF training program acted as a spiritual discipline one could apply anytime when encountering inner turmoil. More than that, the group also praised the *proactive* pastoral counselor's highly-spirited IP, calling him inspiring, and was deemed one of the most significant elements that brought success to the program.

For example, the group described the pastoral counselor as encouraging, compassionate, and sensitive, always seeming to create a sense of trust and compassion within the CIF group. In other words, the integrity of the counselor within the counselor-client relationship paved the way for others to open up, feel safe, and share their life narratives transparently. The following is a short list of comments from the CIF group about the counselor: teacher enthusiasm was excellent, a great educator, speaks clearly, uses the whole Bible, teaches spiritual applications well, can explain the biblical language in a way for lay persons to understand, and is a great dynamic speaker—very captivating and inspiring.

In the final class, one participant mentioned, "Listening to the conflict in others made my eyes open to other people's struggles, which is important to me." Another said, "I have never known any counseling to be like this." Each participant grew in understanding the purpose of pastoral counseling, how not to judge others too soon, and the importance of being open with themselves and others.

The blended tool was an excellent fit for measuring Christian intrapersonal formation in the course. The group responded to the overall process well, enjoyed learning more about themselves spiritually, and blossomed in the group when they felt more secure. The blended tool helped participants identify their spiritual, psychological, and emotional states in a way that created positive responses rather than negative ones. Essentially, the blended tool assessed the overall well-being of each participant while teaching others how to grow toward Christlikeness.

Challenges occurred throughout the program but not with the program itself. Participants experienced commitment issues, such as studying the Scripture each week, being prepared and on time, and feeling good about sharing what they learned about themselves. Most participants had to discover how to overcome how they felt about themselves while trying to overcome their emotions. In short, it took some time for participants to understand the connection between feelings and emotions and how they relate to others during intrapersonal conflict.

The greatest challenge was to get the CIF group members to think biblically. The purpose of the CIF program was to help others decrease intrapersonal conflict by increasing their biblical literacy. By avoiding secular thinking to allow biblical thinking to take over, inner chaos decreases, coping skills strengthen, and self-awareness becomes more stable. Participants finally realized that creating a discipline to help recognize, accept, and manage daily intrapersonal conflict decreases inner chaos, and Christian intrapersonal formation occurs.

Finally, there are two recommendations for future use: provide a formal, preliminary class (Introduction to *Proactive* Pastoral Counseling) to help participants become fully aware of the nature of the class and the commitment required, and extend the time of each class to allow additional conversations to help build and maintain trust in the group sooner. Although this program works for those who believe in Christ, it is recommended for use in helping in other counseling capacities—CBT, CCT, REBT, NT, and SM.

Overall, the CIF small group discovered through firsthand experience with God's Word that one can walk more confidently in Christ and know where to seek help during spiritual struggles. Ultimately, individuals can deepen their daily walk with Christ by consistently engaging with Scripture and practicing spiritual disciplines. This practice enables believers to recognize God's work within them, fostering a more spiritual discernment and a godly perspective on life. As a result, Christian intrapersonal formation becomes a regular part of life, and growth in Christ becomes increasingly evident, even to those wandering still in spiritual darkness.

— 5 —

Conclusion

As Paul describes in 1 Timothy 2:4, God desires everyone to know the truth and be in a relationship with God's Son, Jesus Christ. To better understand the truth, one must begin a spiritually disciplined pursuit by learning to read God's Word, understand God's Word, and apply His Word to one's intrapersonal world. As such, biblical literacy empowers others with the means for conflict resolution, finding rest "in Christ" rather than "in the world" (Matt 11:28–30). As a result, the intrapersonal world of the believer intentionally shifts toward Christlikeness, and internal conflict begins to decrease.[1]

In contrast, Christian intrapersonal formation naturally develops when biblical thinking supersedes secular thinking.[2] For example, incorporating spiritual disciplines in the Bible into daily life fosters spiritual maturity, helping individuals resist worldly pursuits. In 1 John 2:15, John warns, "Do not love the world or the things in the world. If anyone loves the world, the love of the Father is not in him." Therefore, in line with the successes observed

---

1. Timoney, "Identifying the Core Components," 11.
2. Eubanks, *How We Relate*, 167.

through *Proactive* Pastoral Counseling and the Christian Intrapersonal Formation training program, Paul's exhortation in Romans 12:2—to change a culture is to change the way it thinks—proves to be a trustworthy statement.

Unfortunately, the problem is that *Church S* congregants who profess Christianity are too often religion-minded, preference-driven, judgmental, selfish, ritualistic, self-preserving, do not display Christian behavior, and oppose the teaching of the Spirit.[3] Specifically, *Church S* members have too often been unaware when they wrong others, do not understand things of the Spirit, do not seek Christlike change, nor have they been willing to submit to PPC to help them become mature Christians, just as Paul expresses in his second letter to the church in Corinth. Being in that likeness, and according to Paul's proclamation in 2 Corinthians 5:20, "Be reconciled to God," suggests that without the Spirit to discern what dictates sin or the need for forgiveness, *Church S* might never experience Christian intrapersonal formation or the likeness of new life.[4]

Similarly, without the desire to make changes toward Christlikeness, *Church S* might miss out on God's intentions for each other and the purpose of their presence in the *Church S* community. Acts 2:46-47 shows that daily, people broke bread from house to house, ate meals together, expressed sincerity of heart—heart-to-heart conversations (nothing fake)—and praised God communally. Thus, a significant spiritual shift at *Church S* must emerge to create a culture of Christlike discernment.[5]

Therefore, the impetus behind PPC is to help parishioners of *Church S* and all persons and congregations seeking Christian intrapersonal formation to reexamine themselves and the spirit in which their mind operates (see Eph 4:23). The hope of PPC is to assist others to change what they think by helping them change the words they use to process thought. As Paul exhorts in Romans 12:2, "Do not be conformed to this world but be transformed by the renewing

---

3. Pilsbury and Allen, *History of Methodism*, 4.
4. Rainer, *Autopsy of a Deceased Church*, 21–23.
5. Macchia, *Discerning Life*, 126.

Conclusion

of your mind"—cultivate a shift from secular and irrational thinking to thinking biblically.

Many agree that recognizing one's thought process helps one understand how to resolve intrapersonal conflict—applying the correct label to inner turmoil (PPC).[6] From this perspective, and based on this study's results, believers willing to submit to PPC will likely experience spiritual transformation and decrease conflict inwardly. PPC and the CIF program have shown that participants who take their internal strife and "reflect in Christ" realize, more often than not, that intrapersonal conflict stems from the words a person chooses to fuel their cognitive process. In short, words are the culprit of intrapersonal conflict.[7]

Therefore, PPC assumes that intrapersonal conflict decreases from increased spiritually enhanced biblical thinking. As Paul explains in 1 Corinthians 2:12–13, "Now we have received, not the spirit of the world, but the Spirit who is from God, so that we may know the things freely given to us by God, which things we also speak, not in words taught by human wisdom, but in those taught by the Spirit, combining spiritual thoughts with spiritual words."

Pursuing a Christlike mindset sets the stage for yielding fruit from within a Christian culture, making CIF possible. In Proverbs 18:21, King Solomon says, "Death and life are in the power of the tongue, and those who love it will eat its fruit." Keeping that in mind, PPC guides believers into understanding new insights gained from thinking biblically, such as applying and employing those insights for greater spiritual well-being. Ultimately, PPC's overarching goal is to affect the believers' intrapersonal world so that conflict inwardly might be reduced and Christian intrapersonal formation increases.

---

6. Scazzero, *Emotionally Healthy Leader*, 71.
7. McDonald and Walker, "Qualitative Research," 46.

PPC and CIF Implications

This book describes how intrapersonal conflict among participants can be reduced and Christian intrapersonal formation enhanced by substituting secular thinking with biblical thinking. The findings indicate a highly favorable outcome, showing the program's effectiveness in addressing intrapersonal conflict and improving participants' spiritual well-being. Conversely, individuals lacking faith or humility may encounter limitations in their growth. Nonetheless, the results of PPC and the CIF four-step program demonstrate that those open to engaging in *proactive* pastoral counseling will experience significant improvements in cognitive health and authentic Christian intrapersonal formation.

Specifically, CIF helped participants recognize and openly discuss the truth behind their intrapersonal conflict.[8] In a religious culture filled with staunch judgmentalism, safe places to speak openly about deeply profound life occurrences are rare. Essentially, PPC broke through the intolerant spirit of the *Church S* culture with the CIF program by providing participants with an authentic Christian atmosphere to open up about themselves—a place of trust. The CIF small group environment encouraged participants to express old and new truths about their life narratives, and participants grew spiritually from witnessing the testimonies of others.[9] Ultimately, the CIF program allowed others to confront themselves in a way that helped them express and manage internal conflict while safely addressing their feelings and cognitive disruptions more boldly.

In so doing, the CIF program also assisted participants in underlying areas associated with cognitive dissonance. Positive side effects included participants' increased ability to trust others, improved interpersonal communication and self-esteem, inner dialogues shifting from negative to positive self-talk, sharpened ability to discern spiritual things, and having fewer worries about what

---

8. Scazzero, *Emotionally Healthy Leader*, 44.

9. The initial and final interview questions approach each participant from this perspective. In both one-on-one interviews, question three asks, "How do you feel about the 'YOU' in you" that you see right now?

CONCLUSION

others think manifested throughout the program. Empirical results conclude that the CIF program facilitated by the CIT—*Proactive Pastoral Counseling*—helped participants increase biblical literacy, elevate self-awareness, strengthen coping skills, develop a more profound relationship with Christ, and lessen intrapersonal conflict.

Biblical Literacy

One of the most significant aspects of PPC and the CIF training program is its ability to guide others toward biblical literacy. In steps 2 and 3 of the CIF program, "Seek Scripture" and "Scriptural Application," participants become challenged to find cognitive resolve with biblical applications, such as striving for godliness. Paul tells Timothy in 1 Timothy 4:7, "Have nothing to do with worldly fables fit only for old women. On the other hand, discipline yourself for the purpose of godliness."

Unfortunately, the secular world does not consider God or the Bible a valid resource for resolving spiritual matters. As James points out in James 1:4, "You adulteresses, do you not know that friendship with the world is hostility toward God? Therefore, whoever wishes to be a friend of the world makes himself an enemy of God." Yet, herein lies the uniqueness of the CIF training program: CIF relies solely on the Bible and its spiritual applications for resolving intrapersonal conflict, producing spiritual growth and maturity.[10]

Leaf suggests that a believer's changed cognitive faculties enable others to formulate a belief system about life based upon knowing Jesus Christ personally, as revealed in the Bible.[11] Specifically, understanding the biblical Jesus and walking with Him is distinct and must be realized.[12] Therefore, reading the Bible increases one's ability to understand spiritual things (relationship with Christ) only if the person believes what it says and follows its instructions. In Luke 9:23–24, Jesus says, "If anyone wishes to come after Me, he must deny himself, and take up his cross daily

10. Harris, "Christocentric Discipleship," 45–46.
11. Leaf, "Maintaining a Biblical Worldview," 51.
12. Macchia, *Discerning Life*, 80.

and follow Me. For whoever wishes to save his life will lose it, but whoever loses his life for My sake, he is the one who will save it." In short, biblical literacy and CIF are complementary and do not perform outside the other.[13]

Similarly, the essential component of biblical literacy requires a relationship with Christ and acknowledgment of the work of the Holy Spirit.[14] Biblical literacy, then, evolves from Holy Spirit power, empowering one with a deeper meaning behind the Bible story, the ability to discern and apply biblical applications according to God's will for a person's life, and the desire for a deeper relationship with Christ. Morley notes that the gospel of Jesus Christ calls believers to repent, have faith daily, and pursue spiritual disciplines as a grateful response to God's grace.[15] That said, biblical literacy manifests as one gets closer to becoming what God's Word says.

True believers seek nothing less than God's authority and spiritual instructions to rule their world.[16] Essentially, God's Word is His power to man (enforced by the Holy Spirit), enabling believers' peace of mind. Knowing these things reflects one's biblical literacy, spiritual discernment, and ability to find cognitive resolve. Unfortunately, internal interference hinders one's ability to gain Christlike perspectives on how to cope with struggle. Fortunately, CIF intervenes to help others address that conflict.

To achieve this, PPC organizes small group meetings in a safe and supportive environment to address any past or current hurts or confusion that a believer might be experiencing. The CIF training program adopts a nonjudgmental approach within a Christlike atmosphere, encouraging participants to share their internal struggles. PPC finds that intrapersonal conflict is often alleviated through open communication and reading Scripture aloud within the group.[17]

---

13. Rhodes, "Discipling Leadership," 15.
14. Van der Watt, "Mission-Minded Pastoral Theology," 9.
15. Morley, *Man's Guide*, 190.
16. Harris, "Christocentric Discipleship," 17.
17. Marshall and Newheiser, *When Words Matter*, 16.

Conclusion

Furthermore, as individuals become more biblically literate, CIF becomes more effective, decreasing intrapersonal conflict. This internal shift highlights the significance of PPC and CIF training, noting their practical applications. Ultimately, biblical literacy enables believers to understand God's heart more deeply, fostering CIF and paving the way for their hearts and minds to be transformed by His Word (Rom 12:2).

Self Awareness

PPC is an intentional act—pastoral counseling "on wheels"—to engage in a counselor-client relationship with active believers striving for Christlikeness. Using the spiritual infrastructure of the CIF program, PPC inspired others to become more aware of themselves in a manner that produced positive results when looking at one's life, such as realizing new narratives about old stories and people. Some instances proved that although most of the participants in the CIF small group knew each other before the program began, participants learned new things about each other, sometimes changing their perceptions altogether—negative to compassionately positive. PPC proved the CIF training program promotes Christlike self-awareness when implementing an intrapersonal process geared toward biblical literacy and applying spiritual disciplines.[18]

Generally, self-awareness is the ability to see oneself for who they are, incorporating an understanding of one's personality, values, emotions, thoughts, and behaviors.[19] However, self-awareness in Christ is understood best as one paying attention to the presence of God in one's life. Macchia mentions that choosing to live together with intentionality and a growing awareness of God's presence, power, protection, and peace demands a culture change—general self-awareness to self-awareness in Christ.[20] PPC's utilization of

---

18. Stokes, "Heart, Soul, Mind, and Strength," 176.
19. Macchia, *Discerning Life*, 162.
20. Macchia, *Discerning Life*, 162.

the CIF program brings that culture to life, making self-awareness possible in participants willing to allow God to work.[21]

Utilizing the PPC approach, the participants' self-awareness rose by one hundred percent. Each participant gained newfound perspectives on God and how to apply God's Word in one's mind, resulting from participants' increased biblical literacy. Induced by the pastoral counselor's IP, believers became more transparent with themselves because God became to them more than just a reading lesson taken from the Bible—God became to them an authentic, living, and intimate being in their hearts and lives. Incidentally, when participants began to leave at the end of class, some commented on their anticipation for the following week.

While CIF aided in increasing one's frequency of reading the Bible and prayer, PPC also facilitated an understanding of how to apply spiritual disciplines and the purpose of those applications in one's life. One of the most significant realizations the group experienced was that as much as there is a process to growing spiritually, one also naturally employs a cognitive process (default thinking) to inhibit Christlike growth. Step 4 of the CIF program, "Address Irrational Thinking," successfully helped others identify adverse thought processes that inhibit one from pursuing Christlikeness.

For example, when new believers or undiscipled Christians begin thinking about themselves in Christ and moving toward Christlike pursuits, they often struggle to avoid old ways of thinking—biblical thinking takes time. Instead of saying, "I am wonderfully made," one might say to themselves, "I am not worthy of God in my life." From this perspective, participants realized that intrapersonal growth stems from understanding one's negative thought process just as much as acknowledging one's positive process, demonstrating one's pursuit of spiritual maturity. Rhodes comments that spiritual maturity happens when the power of the Holy Spirit begins to transform an individual into becoming more Christlike.[22]

---

21. Hessert, *Introduction to Christianity*, 311.
22. Rhodes, "Discipling Leadership," 12.

Conclusion

In other words, self-awareness alone can often be limited in scope and hinder Christian intrapersonal formation.[23] PPC, however, breaks down the limitations of self-thinking by addressing the words and thoughts one uses that deter them from Christlike thoughts. As a result, participants discovered the origin of their negative thought processes and irrational thinking (adverse thought). In so doing, participants learned to rethink who they are in Christ (not in self), allowing Christlike thinking to move them forward rather than selfish thought (Rom 12:2). In essence, PPC brings biblical thinking versus self-thinking to focus with this statement: "The most extraordinary sense of self-awareness is what comes to mind when a person thinks about God."[24]

Fig. 18. Biblical Thinking vs. Self Thinking (Col 3:1–2)

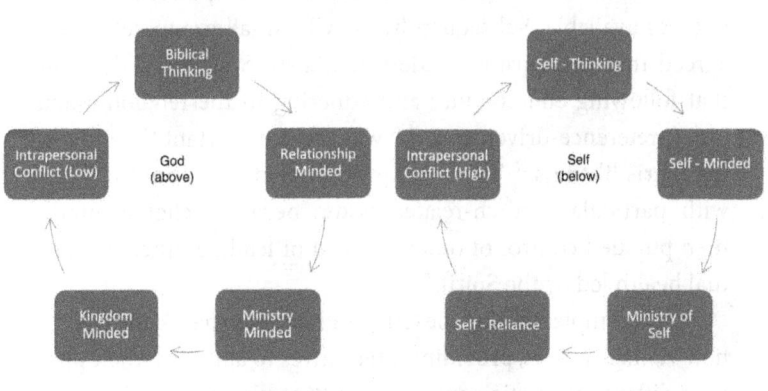

Coping Skills

PPC recognizes coping skills as the necessary components to aid others in managing one's emotions and feelings correctly.[25] By implementing the CIF program, PPC improved the intrapersonal

---

23. Timoney, "Identifying the Core Components," 4.
24. Tozer, *Knowledge of the Holy*, 1.
25. Stokes, "Heart, Soul, Mind, and Strength," 26.

abilities of participants by allowing open discussions on the feelings, thoughts, and emotions of oneself and others experiencing the same struggle. For example, in weeks two through six of the CIF program, participants shared with others for the first time their experiences with the five most common spiritual disruptions within the *Church S* community (Spiritual Leadership, Spiritual Apathy, Lack of Faith, Spiritual Oppression, and Inability to Communicate). As a result, participants learned to recognize, accept, and manage new insights regarding past and present life narratives and beliefs toward themselves and others within the *Church S* culture and community.

Before PPC, members who submitted to the CIF program struggled to manage their spiritual health because there was no one at *Church S* available or spiritually equipped to help them cope with church-related or spiritual issues, as no pastoral counseling was available. Subsequently, the CIF small group collectively agreed that the spiritual leaders at *Church S* enforced the belief that following church rules and adhering to the religious status quo (preference-driven church) was more important than following Christlikeness.[26] The small group noted they could not cope with particular church-related issues because religion-minded men pursued control of others instead of leading others to spiritual health led by the Spirit.[27]

After implementing the CIF program, each participant gained new vantage points, providing alternatives to approach their problems differently. Participants began setting new boundaries,[28] such as learning to say no to irrational thinking, stopping themselves from believing what others might say, standing up for core beliefs, and disciplining themselves to a spiritual growth plan, resulting in an improved ability to communicate interpersonally. Instead of fearing judgment from others, participants began speaking up and speaking out about how they were feeling, raising their self-esteem and values for themselves and others. Overall, PPC intentionally

26. Rainer, *Autopsy of a Deceased Church*, 29.
27. Marshall and Newheiser, *When Words Matter*, 40.
28. Bergman-Pyykkönen et al., "Identities in Motion."

CONCLUSION

engaged participants regarding their intrapersonal conflict from attending *Church S,* making it possible for members to cope better with their spiritual health and to do so when no one is available.

Intrapersonal Conflict

Chapter 2 in this book mentions intrapersonal as being the internal space (cognition) in which a person conducts, deals with, copes, and facilitates rational and irrational thinking. As such, intrapersonal conflict, as laid out in this study, suggests that changes in one's internal space can alter a person's intrapersonal factors, forcing an alternative to rationalize challenging situations or solutions that pertain to the intrapersonal well-being of oneself and others.[29] In other words, this study finds that intrapersonal conflict is nothing more than induced mental chaos in its pursuit of finding cognitive resolve.

In that light, PPC addresses any unresolved cognitive struggles one might experience by illuminating the four self-talk functions of self-criticism, self-reinforcement, self-management, and social assessment.[30] The CIF program provided new insights into intrapersonal chaos, such as where it begins and how to change it. PPC then equipped each participant with the spiritual tools to approach intrapersonal conflict, allowing them to reconsider how they manage their inner chaos. In other words, PPC improved each participant's ability to adjust their thought process from secular thinking to thinking from a biblical standpoint, thereby decreasing intrapersonal conflict. PPC successfully guided others toward clarity in their cognitive processes and facilitated the necessary adjustments for each participant to find mental rest and spiritual resolve in Christ.

---

29. Oleś et al., "Types of Inner Dialogues," 5.
30. Oleś et al., "Types of Inner Dialogues," 4.

Relationship with Christ

PPC and the CIF four-step process are crucial to becoming healthy in one's mind, heart, and spirit.[31] However, the most essential aspect of the CIF program is its ability to help others grow deeper in their relationship with Christ. Utilizing the CIF program, PPC inspired all participants toward a deeper relationship with Christ by directing them to understand the application of Scripture when dealing with intrapersonal struggle.

The evidence shows that Christian intrapersonal formation increases and internal chaos decreases in participants when the Bible is applied. As such, when one's intrapersonal conflict is high (fear of hurt, fear of judgment), biblical literacy is low (self-thinking). When biblical literacy is high, intrapersonal conflict is low in participants. Therefore, a biblically literate person is more prone to cope with intrapersonal issues or when intrapersonal conflict arises (see figure 19).

Fig. 19. Intrapersonal Conflict vs. Biblical Literacy

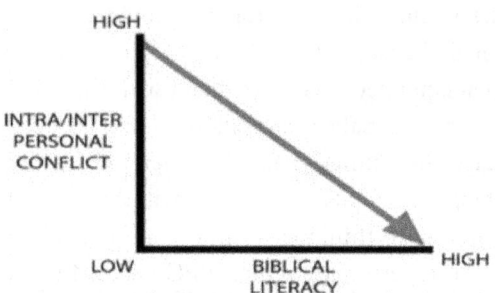

Accordingly, PPC helped improve the spiritual welfare of each participant by assisting them in recognizing individual thought processes, the origin of feelings, how to manage emotions, and how to accurately identify and label the source of intrapersonal conflict.[32] From a biblical perspective, PPC empowered oth-

---

31. Dodson, "Assessing Well-being," 62.
32. Scazzero, *Emotionally Healthy Leader*, 44.

CONCLUSION

ers with a newfound understanding of Christ, leading them out of their current intrapersonal chaos. Participants became renewed by applying spiritual disciplines, such as submitting their thoughts to God's Word and submitting to "Holy Spirit" power for intrapersonal resolve. CIF participants grew more profound in their walk with Christ, realizing that most intrapersonal chaos stems from self-thinking instead of thinking biblically.[33]

Therefore, participants willing to submit to PPC and the CIF program prove that intrapersonal conflict decreases and Christian intrapersonal formation occurs when biblical knowledge increases. As a result, the door for a deeper relationship with Christ opens.

PPC and CIF Applications

One might suggest that PPC, as illustrated through the CIF program, displays the best parts of multiple therapies addressing the cognitive health of others.[34] In other words, therapies like NT, CBT, CCT, REBT, and SM are comparable to PPC. With that in mind, the research applications entailing PPC and the CIF program might come to life more when contrasting the abovementioned therapies' essential tenets (see appendix B).

Most notably, the one component distinguishing PPC from all other therapies (not mentioned above) is its all-encompassing proactive nature. As with other therapies, the term "proactive" means to engage with a client within a session—to challenge irrational thinking.[35] On the other hand, the nature of PPC is *proactive* in itself. In other words, instead of providing pastoral counseling traditionally (reactive counseling), PPC intentionally targets those too timid or hurt to ask for support and helps them confront their issues using a more compassionate, Christlike approach, even when outside the session.

---

33. Oleś et al., "Types of Inner Dialogues," 5.
34. Hawkins and Ohlschlager, "Eclecticism," 468.
35. White, "Conceptualizing Therapy," 99.

In that respect, the evidence concludes that without the guidance of PPC and the CIF program, the six active *Church S* members who submitted to receiving PPC might never have overcome the intrapersonal chaos they experienced in the *Church S* church community and culture. In contrast, all other members at *Church S* who were unwilling to submit to PPC did not experience a decrease in intrapersonal conflict because they refused to pursue the path of Christian intrapersonal formation. Incidentally, those who did not participate in the CIF training program experienced more stress in their personal lives, resulting in more gossip among the other *Church S* members. For a quick glimpse of an in-class session and the results of the CIF four-step process, see appendix A.

PPC and CIF Limitations

PPC benefits all those seeking emotional, spiritual, and intrapersonal health with a desire for a deeper relationship with Christ.[36] As the content of this book displays (although many *Church S* members chose not to submit to PPC), participants of *Church S* who participated in the CIF program significantly improved their lives and overall spiritual well-being. Sara recently commented that out of nowhere, she spontaneously prayed for someone in the hospital where she works—she had never done that before. Edith noted she would never have learned the things she did if it were not for PPC—she now works as a caregiver for a stroke patient. Still, some limitations surfaced regarding the participation of those in the CIF small group, such as the ability of one to accept themselves.[37]

On that note, PPC might not provide the necessary elements for those who experience high levels of psychosis, neurosis, or habitual addictive behaviors. Suppose a person already undergoes therapies that require high doses of medications for medical conditions and require elevated clinical care. In that case, PPC might

---

36. Tan, "Applying Theology," 311.
37. Timoney, "Identifying the Core Components," 4.

CONCLUSION

not meet the clinical requirement for care. Moreover, PPC works best when clients are not forced to participate or attend sessions.

Secondly, implementing PPC in a secular environment might work for some but may not produce the expected results. PPC and the CIF program require faith in Jesus Christ for change to occur. Likewise, without faith, the Holy Spirit cannot work in the individual, nor can the individual understand spiritual things and grow. In other words, intrapersonal conflict becomes overcome by focusing on biblical words and spiritual thoughts taught by the Holy Spirit (1 Cor 2:13). However, PPC cannot dictate the level of growth one might or might not experience under the guidance of PPC.

Third, the participant must be willing to establish a counselor-client relationship. Without the sense of a relationship, the pastoral counselor's IP might not be as effective. The participant may perceive the counselor's approach as having no value. As Matthew says in Matthew 7:6, "Do not give what is holy to dogs and do not throw your pearls before swine, or they will trample them under their feet, and turn and tear you to pieces." If the participant cannot relate to the pastoral counselor on any level, PPC might not best suit the participant, causing an adverse effect and creating more significant intrapersonal conflict.

Fourth, reading text in depth and at length is declining for postmodernism. According to a Pew Research Center survey of US adults conducted from January 25 through February 8, 2021, roughly a quarter of American adults (23 percent) say they have not read a book in whole or in part in the past year, whether in print, electronic, or audio form.[38] One might conclude the Pew Research data suggests that reading is no longer critical due to the vast array of digital applications accessible to the public, such as online video platforms like YouTube, Facebook, and TikTok. With such video platforms, others no longer have to read text to obtain information. Unfortunately, watching online videos might become the norm for future readers seeking to gain information.

Lastly, although the practice of PPC resembles many of the tenets of multiple therapies, PPC might also not best fit those

38. Gelles-Watnick and Perrin, "Who Doesn't Read Books."

experiencing grief or inner pain resulting from loss. PPC can help alleviate some of the thinking one might have to cope with while experiencing the duress of grief; however, the mourning process takes time, and no form of cognitive therapy might work at all.[39] In this case, PPC may work best after an individual's mourning process from losing someone close, limiting the efficacy of its proactive approach initially.

As with many other therapies, examining problems with individuals on a case-by-case basis might help to understand best when to employ PPC despite its limitations. In that light, one must ask if success is due to the program or the individual's effort.[40] In retrospect, PPC is entirely limited if the Holy Spirit is absent.[41]

Conclusion

The contents of this book affirm that all those willing to submit to *Proactive* Pastoral Counseling will minimize intrapersonal chaos while increasing Christian intrapersonal formation. For example, all CIF group members experienced growth in multiple areas (explained earlier), providing great insights into how one's overall spiritual health might become fortified through biblical literacy and the application of spiritual disciplines. However, there are three potential areas to examine for future research.

First, it is essential to know that PPC is a pastoral counseling approach that explicitly targets intrapersonal conflict in believers with biblical thinking. Because faith is a requirement to experience Christian intrapersonal formation,[42] nonbelievers might not be so prone to or interested in enduring the CIF training program. Therefore, future research might examine the effects of the CIF program on nonbelievers (individuals or small groups in a positive environment) experiencing unresolved intrapersonal conflict. In

---

39. Gazzillo et al., "Case Formulation," 115.
40. Timoney, "Identifying the Core Components," 52–53.
41. White, "Conceptualizing Therapy," 95.
42. Leaf, "Maintaining a Biblical Worldview," 50.

Conclusion

so doing, one might inspire unknown disciples to come forward in Christ.[43]

Second, utilizing the CIF program to encourage evangelism and Christlike discipleship (Discipleship Ministries) might benefit Christians and non-Christians alike. Through CIF, trainees become equipped to go out and train others by first learning how to overcome intrapersonal conflict themselves. Whether Christians or non-Christians are on the receiving end, PPC trainees who undergo the CIF training program gain the confidence needed to encourage all people to confront their inner struggles with compassion and genuine care. As a result, CIF reflects the growth in people as they create new disciples through caring for the spiritual needs of others.

Finally, PPC might be successful as a form of pre-counseling for those seeking a better understanding of one's internal being, such as younger couples who might consider marriage—premarital counseling. Maybe a person is taking on a new job and seeks a deeper understanding of one's ability to cope and maintain proper behavior in the workplace. Perhaps a person has never experienced counseling before, does not know what to expect, is embarrassed to talk about individual or family struggles, or is too timid to discover one's failures. These unknowns in a person's life might remain unknown without making PPC and the CIF program available.

In essence, the future of intrapersonal resolve lies not in the hopes of therapies or self-healing ideals.[44] Instead, Christian intrapersonal formation in people relies on *Christlike grit and the power of the Holy Spirit*.[45] PPC might help others rewrite their life stories, replace secular thinking with biblical thinking, and decrease intrapersonal conflict. Still, in the end, the Holy Spirit alone transforms one's story from within, one page at a time.

The future of pastoral counseling may evolve to become more proactive, where counselors actively reach out to individuals

---

43. Van der Watt, "Mission-Minded Pastoral Theology," 7.
44. Tan, "Dealing with Spiritual Struggles," 314.
45. White, "Conceptualizing Therapy," 95.

instead of waiting in an office for clients to seek them out (traditional reactive counseling). In this envisioned future, pastoral counselors might adopt the *proactive* approach of PPC and leverage the CIF training program to engage with those who struggle inwardly, doing so in the name of Christ. Regardless of the future, PPC will continue to use the CIF framework, hoping that others will understand that God's Word is the key to resolving intrapersonal conflict and the driving force behind Christian intrapersonal formation.[46]

---

46. See GraceMinistriesforChrist.org for more information on the author and his ongoing ministry for Christ, to schedule this author for a speaking event for your church or ministry setting, or to learn more about *Proactive Pastoral Counseling* and the Christian Intrapersonal Formation training program.

Appendix A

THE FOLLOWING PRESENTS THE four-step Christian Intrapersonal Formation (CIF) training program along with participant responses from those who engaged in *Proactive* Pastoral Counseling (PPC).

1. Address the Problem: Lack of Spiritual Leadership

   a. What is your problem with the problem?

      - I desire to be spiritually led, but I go home starving for more; no spiritual growth or spiritual growth plan (SPG).
      - I desire godly relationships with others, but members are unwilling to engage with me.

   b. How do you struggle intrapersonally?

      - I want to grow in my faith, but I get nowhere but frustrated.
      - I cannot stop feeling those around me are fake Christians.
      - I feel like I am alone in my walk with Christ.

   c. How does your thinking about the problem affect you?

      - I no longer attend church regularly.
      - I have lost the desire to read my Bible.

Appendix A

- I blame others for how I feel.

2. Seek Scripture: Hebrews 12:1–3

    a. "Therefore, since we have so great a cloud of witnesses surrounding us, let us also lay aside every encumbrance and the sin which so easily entangles us, and let us run with endurance the race that is set before us, fixing our eyes on Jesus, the author and perfecter of faith, who for the joy set before Him endured the cross, despising the shame, and has sat down at the right hand of the throne of God. For consider Him who has endured such hostility by sinners against Himself, so that you will not grow weary and lose heart" (Heb 12:1–3).

    b. How does one overcome intrapersonal conflict?

        - Combine spiritual thoughts with spiritual words taught by the Holy Spirit (1 Cor 2:13). Go to step 3.

3. Apply Spiritual Application(s)

    a. Keep your mind on Christ for godly leadership.

    b. Stay steady in God's Word and do not depend on people for validation.

4. Identify Irrational Thinking

    a. No one likes me.

    b. I am not good enough for others to spend time with me.

    c. Maybe if I change to what they want me to be, I will be good enough for discipleship.

    d. I am not worthy to be a part of their ministry.

    e. I am the problem.

Appendix A

Results

- Increase self-awareness in Christ
- Decrease intrapersonal conflict
- Increase biblical literacy
- Coping skills strengthened (elevated interpersonal communication)
- Deeper walk with Christ

Appendix B
PPC Therapy Comparison List— Proactive *Pastoral Counseling*

Rational Emotional Behavior Therapy (REBT)

Unconditional Self-Acceptance: You are worthy of self-acceptance ✓
Collaborative Empiricism: Testing beliefs against reality ✓
Decatastrophizing: Challenges negative futuristic predictions ✓
Disputing Irrational Beliefs: Replaces beliefs with rational thoughts ✓
Emotional Regulation: Manage emotions by changing thought patterns and beliefs ✓

Christian Cognitive Therapy (CCT)

Biblical Integration: The Bible is the primary source of therapy ✓
Awareness of Thought Patterns: Recognize negative thought ✓
Core Beliefs Examination: Challenges core beliefs ✓
Prayer and Meditation: Encourages clients in spiritual disciplines ✓
Transformation through Christ: No change is possible without the Holy Spirit ✓

Appendix B

Stephen's Ministry (SM)

Ministry for All God's People: Ministry of care is not limited to clergy or professionals	✓
Personal Humility: Humble approach to the ministry	✓
Relational and Caring Skills: Practical skills to connect with others	✓
Spiritual Discernment: Integrates spiritual insights into care	✓
Christ-Centered Care: Committed care that reflects the love of Christ	✓

Cognitive Behavior Therapy (CBT)

Automatic Negative Thoughts: Changing thought patterns lead to emotional improvement	✓
Structured and Time-Based: Goal-oriented	✓
Educative Approach: Teaches others to manage distorted thoughts without aid	✓
Client-Therapist Relationship: Creates active participation in the client	✓
Balanced Outlook: Shifts negative thinking to positive thinking	✓

Narrative Therapy (NT)

Putting Together One's Narrative: Help others construct their life narrative	✓
Unique Outcomes: Widens perspectives by examining alternative stories	✓
Empowerment and Agency: Empowers others with the ability to rewrite narratives	✓
Holistic Application: Considers various life domains—self-esteem, relationships	✓
Narrative as Action: Framing experiences helps engage in the therapeutic process	✓

Appendix C
Proactive Pastoral Counseling Scriptural Foundations

Chapter 1

Exodus

> *Exod 15:8–9*—"And He said, 'I Myself will make all My goodness pass before you, and will proclaim the name of the Lord before you; and I will be gracious to whom I will be gracious, and will show compassion on whom I will show compassion.'"

Gospel of John

> *John 3:8*—"The wind blows where it wishes and you hear the sound of it, but do not know where it comes from and where it is going; so is everyone who is born of the Spirit."

> *John 6:63*—"It is the Spirit who gives life; the flesh profits nothing; the words that I have spoken to you are spirit and are life."

> *John 7:51*—"Our Law does not judge a man unless it first hears from him and knows what he is doing, does it?"

Acts

Acts 7:51—"You men who are stiff-necked and uncircumcised in heart and ears are always resisting the Holy Spirit; you are doing just as your fathers did."

Acts 17:24—"The God who made the world and all things in it, since He is Lord of heaven and earth, does not dwell in temples made with hands."

1 Corinthians

1 Cor 2:2—"And my message and my preaching were not in persuasive words of wisdom, but in demonstration of the Spirit and of power, so that your faith would not rest on the wisdom of men, but on the power of God."

1 Cor 2:11-14—"For who among men knows the thoughts of a man except the spirit of the man which is in him? Even so the thoughts of God no one knows except the Spirit of God. Now we have received, not the spirit of the world, but the Spirit who is from God, so that we may know the things freely given to us by God, which things we also speak, not in words taught by human wisdom, but in those taught by the Spirit, combining spiritual thoughts with spiritual words. But a natural man does not accept the things of the Spirit of God, for they are foolishness to him; and he cannot understand them, because they are spiritually appraised."

1 Cor 11:1—"Be imitators of me, just as I also am of Christ."

2 Corinthians

2 Cor 3:4-6—"Such confidence we have through Christ toward God. Not that we are adequate in ourselves to consider anything as coming from ourselves, but our adequacy is from God, who also made us adequate as servants of a new covenant, not of the letter but of the Spirit; for the letter kills, but the Spirit gives life."

2 Cor 5:19—"God was in Christ reconciling the world to Himself, not counting their trespasses against them, and He has committed to us the word of reconciliation."

2 Cor 10:5—"We are destroying speculations and every lofty thing raised up against the knowledge of God, and we are taking every thought captive to the obedience of Christ."

Ephesians

Eph 4:17-18—"So this I say, and affirm together with the Lord, that you walk no longer just as the Gentiles also walk, in the futility of their mind, being darkened in their understanding, excluded from the life of God because of the ignorance that is in them, because of the hardness of their heart."

Eph 4:22-24—"In reference to your former manner of life, you lay aside the old self, which is being corrupted in accordance with the lusts of deceit, and that you be renewed in the spirit of your mind, and put on the new self, which in the likeness of God has been created in righteousness and holiness of the truth."

Philippians

Phil 2:1-5—"Therefore if there is any encouragement in Christ, if there is any consolation of love, if there is any fellowship of the Spirit, if any affection and compassion, make my joy complete by being of the same mind, maintaining the same love, united in spirit, intent on one purpose. Do nothing from selfishness or empty conceit, but with humility of mind regard one another as more important than yourselves; do not merely look out for your own personal interests, but also for the interests of others. Have this attitude in yourselves which was also in Christ Jesus."

Phil 2:12-13—"So then, my beloved, just as you have always obeyed, not as in my presence only, but now much more in my absence, work out your salvation with fear and trembling; for it is God who is at work in you, both to will and to work for His good pleasure."

1 Thessalonians

1 Thess 2:4—"But just as we have been approved by God to be entrusted with the gospel, so we speak, not as pleasing men, but God who examines our hearts."

1 Thess 5:19—"Do not quench the Spirit."

1 Timothy

1 Tim 4:1-2—"But the Spirit explicitly says that in later times some will fall away from the faith, paying attention to deceitful spirits and doctrines of demons, by means of the hypocrisy of liars seared in their own conscience as with a branding iron."

Hebrews

Heb 3:1-4—"And He is the radiance of His glory and the exact representation of His nature, and upholds all things by the word of His power. When He had made purification of sins, He sat down at the right hand of the Majesty on high, having become as much better than the angels, as He has inherited a more excellent name than they."

Appendix C

Revelation

Rev 3:1-4—"To the angel of the church in Sardis write: He who has the seven Spirits of God and the seven stars, says this: 'I know your deeds, that you have a name that you are alive, but you are dead. Wake up, and strengthen the things that remain, which were about to die; for I have not found your deeds completed in the sight of My God. So remember what you have received and heard; and keep it, and repent. Therefore if you do not wake up, I will come like a thief, and you will not know at what hour I will come to you. But you have a few people in Sardis who have not soiled their garments; and they will walk with Me in white, for they are worthy.'"

Chapter 2

Deuteronomy

Deut 11:18-23—"You shall therefore impress these words of mine on your heart and on your soul; and you shall bind them as a sign on your hand, and they shall be as frontals on your forehead. You shall teach them to your sons, talking of them when you sit in your house and when you walk along the road and when you lie down and when you rise up. You shall write them on the doorposts of your house and on your gates, so that your days and the days of your sons may be multiplied on the land which the Lord swore to your fathers to give them, as long as the heavens remain above the earth. For if you are careful to keep all this commandment which I am commanding you to do, to love the Lord your God, to walk in all His ways and hold fast to Him, then the Lord will drive out all these nations from before you, and you will dispossess nations greater and mightier than you."

Deut 18:15-19—"The Lord your God will raise up for you a prophet like me from among you, from your countrymen, you shall listen to him. This is according to all that you asked of the Lord your God in Horeb on the day of the assembly, saying, 'Let me not hear again the voice of the Lord my God, let me not see this great fire anymore, or I will die.' The Lord said to me, 'They have spoken well. I will raise up a prophet from among their countrymen like you, and I will put My words in his mouth, and he shall speak to them all that I command him. It shall come about that whoever will not listen to My words which he shall speak in My name, I Myself will require it of him.'"

Deut 30:18-20—"I declare to you today that you shall surely perish. You will not prolong your days in the land where you are crossing the Jordan to enter and possess it. I call heaven and earth to witness against you today, that I have set before you life and death, the blessing and the curse. So choose life in order that you may live, you and your descendants, by loving the Lord your God, by obeying His voice, and by holding fast to Him; for this is your life and the length of your days, that you may live in the land which the Lord swore to your fathers, to Abraham, Isaac, and Jacob, to give them."

Psalms

Ps 19:7-14—"The law of the Lord is perfect, restoring the soul; the testimony of the Lord is sure, making wise the simple. The precepts of the Lord are right, rejoicing the heart; the commandment of the Lord is pure, enlightening the eyes. The fear of the Lord is clean, enduring forever; the judgments of the Lord are true; they are righteous altogether. They are more desirable than gold, yes, than much fine gold; sweeter also than honey and the drippings of the honeycomb. Moreover, by them Your servant is warned; in keeping them there is great reward. Who can discern his errors? Acquit me of hidden faults. Also keep back Your servant from presumptuous sins; let them not rule over me; then I will be blameless, and I shall be acquitted of great transgression. Let the words of my mouth and the meditation of my heart be acceptable in Your sight, O Lord, my rock and my Redeemer."

Ps 81:11—"But My people did not listen to My voice, and Israel did not obey Me."

Proverbs

Prov 2:1-5—"My son, if you will receive my words and treasure my commandments within You. Make your ear attentive to wisdom, incline your heart to understanding; for if you cry for discernment, lift your voice for understanding; if you seek her as silver and search for her as for hidden treasures; then you will discern the fear of the Lord and discover the knowledge of God."

Prov 23:12—"Apply your heart to discipline and your ears to words of knowledge."

Isaiah

Isa 46:10—"Declaring the end from the beginning, and from ancient times things which have not been done, saying, 'My purpose will be established, And I will accomplish all My good pleasure.'"

Gospel of Matthew

Matt 4:4—"But He answered and said, 'It is written, man shall not live on bread alone, but on every word that proceeds out of the mouth of God.'"

Matt 5:1-2—"When Jesus saw the crowds, He went up on the mountain; and after He sat down, His disciples came to Him. He opened His mouth and began to teach them."

Luke

Luke 9:23—"And He was saying to them all, 'If anyone wishes to come after Me, he must deny himself, and take up his cross daily and follow Me.'"

Luke 9:35—"Then a voice came out of the cloud, saying, 'This is My Son, My Chosen One; listen to Him!'"

Luke 24:27—"Then beginning with Moses and with all the prophets, He explained to them the things concerning Himself in all the Scriptures."

Gospel of John

John 1:3-4—"All things came into being through Him, and apart from Him nothing came into being that has come into being. In Him was life, and the life was the Light of men."

John 1:14—"And the Word became flesh, and dwelt among us, and we saw His glory, glory as of the only begotten from the Father, full of grace and truth."

John 1:17—"For the Law was given through Moses; grace and truth were realized through Jesus Christ."

John 4:14—"But whoever drinks of the water that I will give him shall never thirst; but the water that I will give him will become in him a well of water springing up to eternal life."

John 4:22—"You worship what you do not know; we worship what we know, for salvation is from the Jews."

John 6:53-58—"So Jesus said to them, 'Truly, truly, I say to you, unless you eat the flesh of the Son of Man and drink His blood, you have no life in yourselves. He who eats My flesh and drinks My blood has eternal life, and I will raise him up on the last day. For My flesh is true food, and My blood is true drink. He who eats My flesh and drinks My blood abides in Me, and I in him. As the Living Father sent Me, and I live because of the Father, so he who eats Me, he also will live

Appendix C

because of Me. This is the bread which came down out of heaven; not as the fathers ate and died; he who eats this bread will live forever.'"

John 6:63—"It is the Spirit who gives life; the flesh profits nothing; the words that I have spoken to you are spirit and are life."

John 8:12—"Then Jesus again spoke to them, saying, 'I am the Light of the world; he who follows Me will not walk in the darkness, but will have the Light of life.'"

John 11:25-26—"Jesus said to her, 'I am the resurrection and the life; he who believes in Me will live even if he dies, and everyone who lives and believes in Me will never die. Do you believe this?'"

John 14:6—"Jesus said to him, 'I am the way, and the truth, and the life; no one comes to the Father but through Me.'"

John 15:12—"This is My commandment, that you love one another, just as I have loved you."

Acts

Acts 9:6—"But get up and enter the city, and it will be told you what you must do."

Acts 9:18-20—"And immediately there fell from his eyes something like scales, and he regained his sight, and he got up and was baptized; and he took food and was strengthened. Now for several days he was with the disciples who were at Damascus, and immediately he began to proclaim Jesus in the synagogues, saying, 'He is the Son of God.'"

Acts 17:28—"For in Him we live and move and exist, as even some of your own poets have said, 'For we also are His children.'"

Appendix C

Romans

Rom 8:1—"Therefore there is now no condemnation for those who are in Christ Jesus."

Rom 8:6-8—"For the mind set on the flesh is death, but the mind set on the Spirit is life and peace, because the mind set on the flesh is hostile toward God; for it does not subject itself to the law of God, for it is not even able to do so, and those who are in the flesh cannot please God."

Rom 10:9-10—"If you confess with your mouth Jesus as Lord, and believe in your heart that God raised Him from the dead, you will be saved; for with the heart a person believes, resulting in righteousness, and with the mouth he confesses, resulting in salvation."

Rom 12:2—"Do not be conformed to this world, but be transformed by the renewing of your mind, so that you may prove what the will of God is, that which is good and acceptable and perfect."

Rom 7:14-25—"For we know that the Law is spiritual, but I am of flesh, sold into bondage to sin. For what I am doing, I do not understand; for I am not practicing what I would like to do, but I am doing the very thing I hate. But if I do the very thing I do not want to do, I agree with the Law, confessing that the Law is good. So now, no longer am I the one doing it, but sin which dwells in me. For I know that nothing good dwells in me, that is, in my flesh; for the willing is present in me, but the doing of the good is not. For the good that I want, I do not do, but I practice the very evil that I do not want. But if I am doing the very thing I do not want, I am no longer the one doing it, but sin which dwells in me. I find then the principle that evil is present in me, the one who wants to do good. For I joyfully concur with the law of God in the inner man, but I see a different law in the members of my body, waging war against the law of my mind and making me a prisoner of the law of sin which is in my members. Wretched man that I am! Who will set me free from the body of this death? Thanks be to God through Jesus Christ our Lord! So then, on the one hand I myself with my mind am serving the law of God, but on the other, with my flesh the law of sin."

1 Corinthians

1 Cor 1:12-13—"Now I mean this, that each one of you is saying, 'I am of Paul,' and 'I of Apollos,' and 'I of Cephas,' and 'I of Christ.' Has Christ been divided? Paul was not crucified for you, was he? Or were you baptized in the name of Paul?"

1 Cor 1:18—"For the word of the cross is foolishness to those who are perishing, but to us who are being saved it is the power of God."

1 Cor 6:11-12—"Such were some of you; but you were washed, but you were sanctified, but you were justified in the name of the Lord Jesus Christ and in the Spirit of our God. All things are lawful for me, but not all things are profitable. All things are lawful for me, but I will not be mastered by anything."

2 Corinthians

2 Cor 5:14-17—"For the love of Christ controls us, having concluded this, that one died for all, therefore all died; and He died for all, so that they who live might no longer live for themselves, but for Him who died and rose again on their behalf. Therefore from now on we recognize no one according to the flesh; even though we have known Christ according to the flesh, yet now we know Him in this way no longer. Therefore if anyone is in Christ, he is a new creature; the old things passed away; behold, new things have come."

2 Cor 10:5—"We are destroying speculations and every lofty thing raised up against the knowledge of God, and we are taking every thought captive to the obedience of Christ."

Appendix C

2 Cor 12:9—"And He has said to me, 'My grace is sufficient for you, for power is perfected in weakness.' Most gladly, therefore, I will rather boast about my weaknesses, so that the power of Christ may dwell in me."

Galatians

Gal 5:16—"But I say, walk by the Spirit, and you will not carry out the desire of the flesh."

Ephesians

Eph 4:22-24—"In reference to your former manner of life, you lay aside the old self, which is being corrupted in accordance with the lusts of deceit, and that you be renewed in the spirit of your mind, and put on the new self, which in the likeness of God has been created in righteousness and holiness of the truth."

Philippians

Phil 2:8-11—"Being found in appearance as a man, He humbled Himself by becoming obedient to the point of death, even death on a cross. For this reason also, God highly exalted Him, and bestowed on Him the name which is above every name, so that at the name of Jesus every knee will bow, of those who are in heaven and on earth and under the earth, and that every tongue will confess that Jesus Christ is Lord, to the glory of God the Father."

Phil 4:7—"And the peace of God, which surpasses all comprehension, will guard your hearts and your minds in Christ Jesus."

Appendix C

Colossians

Col 3:1-2—"Therefore if you have been raised up with Christ, keep seeking the things above, where Christ is, seated at the right hand of God. Set your mind on the things above, not on the things that are on earth."

1 Timothy

1 Tim 2:3-4—"This is good and acceptable in the sight of God our Savior, who desires all men to be saved and to come to the knowledge of the truth."

1 Tim 4:6-7—"In pointing out these things to the brethren, you will be a good servant of Christ Jesus, constantly nourished on the words of the faith and of the sound doctrine which you have been following. But have nothing to do with worldly fables fit only for old women. On the other hand, discipline yourself for the purpose of godliness."

2 Timothy

2 Tim 3:16-17—"All Scripture is inspired by God and profitable for teaching, for reproof, for correction, for training in righteousness; so that the man of God may be adequate, equipped for every good work."

Hebrews

Heb 1:2-4—"In these last days has spoken to us in His Son, whom He appointed heir of all things, through whom also He made the world. And He is the radiance of His glory and the exact representation of His nature, and upholds all things by the word of His power. When He had made purification of sins, He sat down at the right hand of the Majesty on high, having become as much better than the angels, as He has inherited a more excellent name than they."

James

Jas 1:21—"Therefore, putting aside all filthiness and all that remains of wickedness, in humility receive the word implanted, which is able to save your souls."

Chapter 3

Proverbs

Prov 3:5–6—"Trust in the Lord with all your heart and do not lean on your own understanding. In all your ways acknowledge Him, and He will make your paths straight."

Gospel of Mark

Mark 12:31—"The second is this, 'You shall love your neighbor as yourself.' There is no other commandment greater than these."

Gospel of Luke

Luke 9:23—"And He was saying to them all, 'If anyone wishes to come after Me, he must deny himself, and take up his cross daily and follow Me.'"

2 Corinthians

2 Cor 5:18–20—"Now all these things are from God, who reconciled us to Himself through Christ and gave us the ministry of reconciliation, namely, that God was in Christ reconciling the world to Himself, not counting their trespasses against them, and He has committed to us the word of reconciliation. Therefore, we are ambassadors for Christ, as though God were making an appeal through us; we beg you on behalf of Christ, be reconciled to God."

Ephesians

Eph 4:32—"Be kind to one another, tender-hearted, forgiving each other, just as God in Christ also has forgiven you."

Chapter 4

Nehemiah

Neh 6:1–8—"Now when it was reported to Sanballat, Tobiah, to Geshem the Arab and to the rest of our enemies that I had rebuilt the wall, and that no breach remained in it, although at that time I had not set up the doors in the gates, then Sanballat and Geshem sent a message to me, saying, 'Come, let us meet together at Chephirim in the plain of Ono.' But they were planning to harm me. So I sent messengers to them, saying, 'I am doing a great work and I cannot come down. Why should the work stop while I leave it and come down to you?' They sent messages to me four times in this manner, and I answered them in the same way. Then Sanballat sent his servant to me in the same manner a fifth time with an open letter in his hand. In it was written, 'It is reported among the nations, and Gashmu says, that you and the Jews are planning to rebel; therefore you are rebuilding the wall. And you are to be their king, according to these reports. You have also appointed prophets to proclaim in Jerusalem concerning you, "A king is in Judah!" And now it will be reported to the king according to these reports. So come now, let us take counsel together.' Then I sent a message to him saying, 'Such things as you are saying have not been done, but you are inventing them in your own mind.'"

Appendix C

Psalms

Ps 62:1-2—"My soul waits in silence for God only; from Him is my salvation. He only is my rock and my salvation, my stronghold; I shall not be greatly shaken."

Ps 118:8—"It is better to take refuge in the Lord than to trust in man."

Proverbs

Prov 3:5-6—"Trust in the Lord with all your heart and do not lean on your own understanding. In all your ways acknowledge Him, and He will make your paths straight."

Isaiah

Isa 40:31—"Yet those who wait for the Lord will gain new strength; they will mount up with wings like eagles, they will run and not get tired, they will walk and not become weary."

Gospel of Matthew

Matt 10:31—"So do not fear; you are more valuable than many sparrows."

Matt 11:28-30—"Come to Me, all who are weary and heavy-laden, and I will give you rest. Take My yoke upon you and learn from Me, for I am gentle and humble in heart, and you will find rest for your souls. For My yoke is easy and My burden is light."

Gospel of Luke

Luke 9:23—"And He was saying to them all, 'If anyone wishes to come after Me, he must deny himself, and take up his cross daily and follow Me.'"

Luke 10:19—"Behold, I have given you authority to tread on serpents and scorpions, and over all the power of the enemy, and nothing will injure you."

Acts

Acts 20:22—"And now, behold, bound by the Spirit, I am on my way to Jerusalem, not knowing what will happen to me there."

Romans

Rom 8:5—"For those who are according to the flesh set their minds on the things of the flesh, but those who are according to the Spirit, the things of the Spirit."

Rom 10:17—"So faith comes from hearing, and hearing by the word of Christ."

Rom 12:2—"And do not be conformed to this world, but be transformed by the renewing of your mind, so that you may prove what the will of God is, that which is good and acceptable and perfect."

2 Corinthians

2 Cor 5:17—"Therefore if anyone is in Christ, he is a new creature; the old things passed away; behold, new things have come."

2 Cor 10:4-5—"For the weapons of our warfare are not of the flesh, but divinely powerful for the destruction of fortresses. We are destroying speculations and every lofty thing raised up against the knowledge of God, and we are taking every thought captive to the obedience of Christ."

Galatians

Gal 5:16–18—"But I say, walk by the Spirit, and you will not carry out the desire of the flesh. For the flesh sets its desire against the Spirit, and the Spirit against the flesh; for these are in opposition to one another, so that you may not do the things that you please. But if you are led by the Spirit, you are not under the Law."

Ephesians

Eph 4:22–24—"In reference to your former manner of life, you lay aside the old self, which is being corrupted in accordance with the lusts of deceit, and that you be renewed in the spirit of your mind, and put on the new self, which in the likeness of God has been created in righteousness and holiness of the truth."

Eph 6:10–17—"Finally, be strong in the Lord and in the strength of His might. Put on the full armor of God, so that you will be able to stand firm against the schemes of the devil. For our struggle is not against flesh and blood, but against the rulers, against the powers, against the world forces of this darkness, against the spiritual forces of wickedness in the heavenly places. Therefore, take up the full armor of God, so that you will be able to resist in the evil day, and having done everything, to stand firm. Stand firm therefore, having girded your loins with truth, and having put on the breastplate of righteousness, and having shod your feet with the preparation of the gospel of peace; in addition to all, taking up the shield of faith with which you will be able to extinguish all the flaming arrows of the evil one. And take the helmet of salvation, and the sword of the Spirit, which is the word of God."

Philippians

Phil 4:8—"Finally, brethren, whatever is true, whatever is honorable, whatever is right, whatever is pure, whatever is lovely, whatever is of good repute, if there is any excellence and if anything worthy of praise, dwell on these things."

1 Timothy

1 Tim 4:1-2—"But the Spirit explicitly says that in later times some will fall away from the faith, paying attention to deceitful spirits and doctrines of demons, by means of the hypocrisy of liars seared in their own conscience as with a branding iron."

2 Timothy

2 Tim 3:14-17—"You, however, continue in the things you have learned and become convinced of, knowing from whom you have learned them, and that from childhood you have known the sacred writings which are able to give you the wisdom that leads to salvation through faith which is in Christ Jesus. All Scripture is inspired by God and profitable for teaching, for reproof, for correction, for training in righteousness; so that the man of God may be adequate, equipped for every good work."

Hebrews

Heb 11:1—"Now faith is the assurance of things hoped for, the conviction of things not seen."

James

Jas 1:19-21—"This you know, my beloved brethren. But everyone must be quick to hear, slow to speak and slow to anger; for the anger of man does not achieve the righteousness of God. Therefore, putting aside all filthiness and all that remains of wickedness, in humility receive the word implanted, which is able to save your souls."

1 Peter

1 Pet 5:6-7—"Therefore humble yourselves under the mighty hand of God, that He may exalt you at the proper time, casting all your anxiety on Him, because He cares for you."

1 John

1 John 3:21—"Beloved, if our heart does not condemn us, we have confidence before God."

Chapter 5

Proverbs

Prov 18:21—"Death and life are in the power of the tongue, and those who love it will eat its fruit."

Gospel of Matthew

Matt 7:6—"Do not give what is holy to dogs, and do not throw your pearls before swine, or they will trample them under their feet, and turn and tear you to pieces."

Matt 11:28-30—"Come to Me, all who are weary and heavy-laden, and I will give you rest. Take My yoke upon you and learn from Me, for I am gentle and humble in heart, and you will find rest for your souls. For My yoke is easy and My burden is light."

Gospel of Luke

Luke 9:23-24—"And He was saying to them all, 'If anyone wishes to come after Me, he must deny himself, and take up his cross daily and follow Me. For whoever wishes to save his life will lose it, but whoever loses his life for My sake, he is the one who will save it.'"

Acts

Acts 2:46-47—"Day by day continuing with one mind in the temple, and breaking bread from house to house, they were taking their meals together with gladness and sincerity of heart, praising God and having favor with all the people. And the Lord was adding to their number day by day those who were being saved."

Acts 17:28—"For in Him we live and move and exist, as even some of your own poets have said, 'For we also are His children.'"

Romans

Rom 12:2—"And do not be conformed to this world, but be transformed by the renewing of your mind, so that you may prove what the will of God is, that which is good and acceptable and perfect."

1 Corinthians

1 Cor 2:12-13—"Now we have received, not the spirit of the world, but the Spirit who is from God, so that we may know the things freely given to us by God, which things we also speak, not in words taught by human wisdom, but in those taught by the Spirit, combining spiritual thoughts with spiritual words."

2 Corinthians

2 Cor 2:12-15—"Now when I came to Troas for the gospel of Christ and when a door was opened for me in the Lord, I had no rest for my spirit, not finding Titus my brother; but taking my leave of them, I went on to Macedonia. But thanks be to God, who always leads us in triumph in Christ, and manifests through us the sweet aroma of the knowledge of Him in every place. For we are a fragrance of Christ to God among those who are being saved and among those who are perishing."

2 Cor 5:20—"Therefore, we are ambassadors for Christ, as though God were making an appeal through us; we beg you on behalf of Christ, be reconciled to God."

Ephesians

Eph 4:22-24—"In reference to your former manner of life, you lay aside the old self, which is being corrupted in accordance with the lusts of deceit, and that you be renewed in the spirit of your mind, and put on the new self, which in the likeness of God has been created in righteousness and holiness of the truth."

Colossians

Col 3:1-2—"Therefore if you have been raised up with Christ, keep seeking the things above, where Christ is, seated at the right hand of God. Set your mind on the things above, not on the things that are on earth."

Appendix C

1 Timothy

1 Tim 2:3–4—"This is good and acceptable in the sight of God our Savior, who desires all men to be saved and to come to the knowledge of the truth."

1 Tim 4:7—"But have nothing to do with worldly fables fit only for old women. On the other hand, discipline yourself for the purpose of godliness."

James

Jas 1:4—"And let endurance have its perfect result, so that you may be perfect and complete, lacking in nothing."

1 John

1 John 2:15—"Do not love the world nor the things in the world. If anyone loves the world, the love of the Father is not in him."

Bibliography

Aadne, Linda. "Radical Discipleship in Participation: Spiritual Formation in Baptist Community." *Journal of European Baptist Studies* 22 (2022) 77–96.

Ahonle, Zaccheus J., et al. "The 2023 Revision to the CRCC Code of Ethics: Implications for Defining and Protecting the Counselor-Client Relationship." *Rehabilitation Counseling Bulletin* 66 (2023) 257–64.

Anderson, Tawa J., et al. *An Introduction to Christian Worldview: Pursuing God's Perspective in a Pluralistic World.* Downers Grove, IL: InterVarsity, 2017.

Bergman-Pyykkönen, Marina, et al. "Identities in Motion: Boundary-Crossing Learning from an Intrapersonal Perspective." *Learning, Culture and Social Interaction* 44 (2023). https://doi.org/10.1016/j.lcsi.2023.100780.

Brooks, Jeanne. "Cognitive-Behavior Therapy." In *The Popular Encyclopedia of Christian Counseling: An Indispensable Tool for Helping People with Their Problems.* Edited by Tim Clinton and Ron Hawkins. Eugene, OR: Harvest House, 2011.

Brunt, R. J. "The Role of Embodied Cognition in Performing the Word of God." *Journal of Psychology and Christianity* 35 (2016) 242–53.

Bulteau, Samuel, et al. "The Update of Self-Identity: Importance of Assessing Autobiographical Memory in Major Depressive Disorder." *Wiley Interdisciplinary Review Cognitive Science* 14.3 (2023) 1–10.

Campbell, William S. *Romans: A Social Identity Commentary.* London: T&T Clark, 2023.

Carlson, Gregory C. "Adult Development and Christian Formation." In *Christian Formation: Integrating Theology and Human Development.* Edited by James R. Estep and Jonathan H. Kim. Nashville: B&H, 2010.

Carson, D. A. *The Gospel According to John.* Grand Rapids: Eerdmans, 1991.

Cheng, Albert, et al. "The Development and Validation of the Practicing Faith Survey." *Journal of Psychology and Theology* 51 (2023) 67–86.

Cockerill, Gareth L. *The Epistle to the Hebrews.* Edited by Ned. B. Stonehouse et al. Grand Rapids: Eerdmans, 2012.

Bibliography

Cox, William F., Jr., and Robert A. Peck. "Christian Education as Discipleship Formation." *Christian Education Journal* 15 (2018) 243–61.

Crabb, Larry. *Effective Biblical Counseling: A Model for Helping Caring Christians Become Capable Counselors.* Grand Rapids: Zondervan, 2013.

Dodson, Neil B. "Assessing Well-Being in a Pastoral Counseling Program." In *Scholars Crossing Doctoral Dissertations and Projects.* PhD diss., John W. Rawlings School of Divinity, 2021.

Eubanks, Jesse. *How We Relate: Understanding God, Yourself, and Others Through the Enneagram.* Grand Rapids: Zondervan, 2023.

Fischer, David Hackett. *Albion's Seed: Four British Folkways in America.* New York: Oxford University Press, 1989.

Freedman, Jill. "Feelings, Thinking and Action as a Coherent Whole: A Reflection on 'Traveling Down the Neuro-Pathway.'" *International Journal of Narrative Therapy and Community Work* 3 (2019) 61–63.

Garland, David E. *Luke.* Edited by Clinton E. Arnold. Zondervan Exegetical Commentary Series on the New Testament, vol. 3. Grand Rapids: HarperCollins, 2011.

Garzon, Fernando. "Lay Counseling." In *The Popular Encyclopedia of Christian Counseling: An Indispensable Tool for Helping People with Their Problems.* Edited by Tim Clinton and Ron Hawkins. Eugene, OR: Harvest House, 2011.

Gazzillo, Francesco, et al. "Case Formulation and Treatment Planning: How to Take Care of Relationship and Symptoms Together." *Journal of Psychotherapy Integration* 40 (2021) 115–28.

Gelles-Watnick, Risa, and Andrew Perrin. "Who Doesn't Read Books in America?" Pew Research Center, Sept. 21, 2021. https://www.pewresearch.org/short-reads/2021/09/21/who-doesnt-read-books-in-america/.

Guo, Xiuyan, et al. "Development and Validation of the Peer Assessment Motivation Scale (PAMS) in Higher Education." *Studies in Higher Education* 48 (2023) 1243–57.

Harris, Allan Clyde, II. "Christocentric Discipleship at Faith Baptist Church of Tuscola." In *Scholars Crossing Doctoral Dissertations and Projects.* PhD diss., John W. Rawlings School of Divinity, 2023.

Haugk, Kenneth. *Stephen Ministry Training Manual.* Vol. 1. St. Louis: Stephen Ministries, 2000.

Hawkins, Ron, and George Ohlschlager. "Eclecticism." In *The Popular Encyclopedia of Christian Counseling: An Indispensable Tool for Helping People with Their Problems.* Edited by Tim Clinton and Ron Hawkins. Eugene, OR: Harvest House, 2011.

Haykin, Michael A. G. *The God Who Draws Near: An Introduction to Biblical Spirituality.* Webster, NY: Evangelical Press, 2020.

Hessert, Paul. *Introduction to Christianity.* New York: Taylor & Francis, 2023.

Hill, Marcy. "Integrative Narrative Therapy in Counseling: Experiencing Strengthened Spiritual Resiliency; A Phenomenological Study." In *Scholars*

BIBLIOGRAPHY

Crossing Doctoral Dissertations and Projects. PhD diss., John W. Rawlings School of Divinity, 2020.
Hinson, Victor. "Integrationist Perspective." In *The Popular Encyclopedia of Christian Counseling: An Indispensable Tool for Helping People with Their Problems.* Edited by Tim Clinton and Ron Hawkins. Eugene, OR: Harvest House, 2011.
Issler, Klaus. *Living in the Life of Jesus: The Formation of Christian Character.* Downers Grove, IL: InterVarsity, 2012.
Jamieson, Philip. "Narrative Therapy." In *The Popular Encyclopedia of Christian Counseling: An Indispensable Tool for Helping People with Their Problems.* Edited by Tim Clinton and Ron Hawkins. Eugene, OR: Harvest House, 2011.
Knight, Anita. "Rogerian Therapy." In *The Popular Encyclopedia of Christian Counseling: An Indispensable Tool for Helping People with Their Problems.* Edited by Tim Clinton and Ron Hawkins. Eugene, OR: Harvest House, 2011.
Koester, Craig. *Hebrews: A New Translation with Introduction and Commentary.* Anchor Yale Bible, vol. 36. New Haven: Yale University Press, 2008.
Leaf, Scott. "Maintaining a Biblical Worldview: Mitigating Emerging Syncretism with Worldly Philosophies Through Focused Instruction in Christian Theology." In *Scholars Crossing Doctoral Dissertations and Projects.* PhD diss., John W. Rawlings School of Divinity, 2021.
Leins, Chris J. K. "What Makes Pastoral Counseling So Pastoral? Distinguishing Between Pastoral Care and Clinical Practice in Modern Life." *Journal of Psychology and Christianity* 40 (2021) 344–56.
Liu, Yanhong, et al. "Counselor Trainees' Personal Growth Through Interpersonal Experiential Growth Groups: An Instrumental Case Study." *Journal of Counselor Preparation and Supervision* 14.4 (2021) 1–32.
Louw, D. J. "A Christian Spirituality of Imperfection: Towards a Pastoral Theology of Descent Within the Praxis of Orthopathy." *Acta Theologica* 41.2 (2021) 70–95.
Macchia, Stephen. *The Discerning Life: An Invitation to Notice God in Everything.* Grand Rapids: Zondervan, 2022.
Maddix, Mark A. "Spiritual Formation and Christian Formation." In *Christian Formation: Integrating Theology and Human Development.* Edited by James R. Estep and Jonathan H. Kim. Nashville: B&H, 2010.
Marshall, Cheryl, and Caroline Newheiser. *When Words Matter Most: Speaking Truth with Grace to Those You Love.* Wheaton, IL: Crossway, 2021.
Marshall, Howard. *The Gospel of Luke: A Commentary on the Greek Text.* Grand Rapids: Eerdmans, 1978.
Mayo Clinic. "Persistent Depressive Disorder." Dec. 2, 2022. https://www.mayoclinic.org/diseases-conditions/persistent-depressive-disorder/symptoms-causes/syc-20350929.

BIBLIOGRAPHY

———. "Seasonal Affective Disorder (SAD)." Dec. 14, 2021. https://www.mayoclinic.org/diseases-conditions/seasonal-affective-disorder/symptoms-causes/syc-20364651.

McClendon, P. Adam. *Paul's Spirituality in Galatians: A Critique of Contemporary Christian Spiritualities*. Eugene, OR: Wipf and Stock, 2015.

McDonald, Kari, and Lorraine Walker. "Qualitative Research on Self-Transcendence in Older Adults: A Scoping Review." *Journal of Gerontological Nursing* 49.9 (2023) 43–48.

McKinney, Lori-Ellen. *Christian Education in the African American Church: A Guide for Teaching Truth*. Valley Forge, PA: Judson, 2003.

McMinn, Mark R., and Clark D. Campbell. *Integrative Psychotherapy: Toward a Comprehensive Christian Approach*. Downers Grove, IL: InterVarsity, 2007.

Millet, Joshua, *A History of the Baptists in Maine and a Dictionary of the Labors of Each Minister*. Portland, ME: Charles Day, 1845.

Moo, Douglas J. *The Epistle to the Romans*. Grand Rapids: Eerdmans, 1996.

Moorey, Stirling. "Three Ways to Change Your Mind: An Epistemic Framework for Cognitive Interventions." *Behavioral and Cognitive Psychotherapy* 51 (2023) 187–99.

Morley, Patrick. *A Man's Guide to the Spiritual Disciplines: 12 Habits to Strengthen Your Walk with Christ*. Chicago: Moody, 2023.

Moschella, M. C. "Affect in Narrative Spiritual Care." *Pastoral Psychology* 73.2 (2023) 151–62.

Murray, Andrew. *Humility: The Beauty of Holiness*. New York: Revell, 1895.

Okeke, Nkechi Mercy, et al. "Effect of a Religious Coping Intervention of Rational Emotive Behavior Therapy on Mental Health of Adult Learners with Type II Diabetes." *Medicine (Baltimore)* 102.39 (2023) 1–10. http://dx.doi.org/10.1097/MD.0000000000034485.

Oleś, Piotr K., et al. "Types of Inner Dialogues and Functions of Self-Talk: Comparisons and Implications." *Frontiers in Psychology* 11 (2020) 1–13. https://doi.org/10.3389/fpsyg.2020.00227.

Ortberg, John. *The Me I Want to Be: Becoming God's Best Version of You*. Grand Rapids: Zondervan, 2010.

Pearl, Michael. *Understanding the Book of Hebrews: A Word by Word Commentary*. Pleasantville, TN: No Greater Joy Ministries, 2021.

Pilsbury, W. H., and Stephen Allen. *History of Methodism in Maine*. Augusta, ME: Charles E. Nash, 1887.

Pramanik, Suchismita, and Rooplekha Khuntia. "Decoding Unconditional Self-Acceptance: A Qualitative Report." *Journal of Rational Cognitive-Behavior Therapy* 15.1 (2023) 1–18.

Psychology Today. "Rational Emotive Behavior Therapy." Last modified July 27, 2022. https://www.psychologytoday.com/us/therapy-types/rational-emotive-behavior-therapy.

Rainer, Thom S. *Autopsy of a Deceased Church: 12 Ways to Keep Yours Alive*. Nashville: B&H, 2014.

Bibliography

Rhodes, Jerry A. "Discipling Leadership Is Key to Church Revitalization: A Revitalization Strategy for Declining Churches." In *Scholars Crossing Doctoral Dissertations and Projects*. PhD diss., John W. Rawlings School of Divinity, 2022.

Rice, Dwight. "Story Tuning: Growing in Favor with God in the Midst of Relationships." Video lecture in PACO 825 course. Lynchburg, VA: Liberty University, 2022.

———. "Subject Matter Conversations: Initial." Video lecture in PACO 825 course. Lynchburg, VA: Liberty University, 2022.

Scazzero, Peter. *The Emotionally Healthy Leader: How Transforming Your Inner Life Will Deeply Transform Your Church, Team, and the World*. Grand Rapids: Zondervan, 2015.

Sensing, Timothy R. *Qualitative Research: A Multi-Methods Approach to Projects for Doctor of Ministry Theses*. Eugene, OR: Wipf & Stock, 2011.

Setran, David P., and Jim Wilhoit. "Christian Education and Spiritual Formation: Recent History and Future Prospects." *Christian Education Journal* 17 (2020) 530–46.

Sleeper, C. Freeman. *James*. Abingdon New Testament Commentaries. Nashville: Abingdon, 1998.

Sproul, R. C. "3 Types of Legalism." Ligonier Ministries, July 17, 2019. https://www.ligonier.org/learn/articles/3-types-legalism.

Spurgeon, Charles. *Lectures to My Students*. Grand Rapids: Zondervan, 1954.

Stephen Ministries. "What Is Stephen Ministry?" https://www.stephenministries.org/stephenministry/default.cfm/917?mnb=1.

Stokes, Christopher T. "Heart, Soul, Mind, and Strength: Understanding Spirituality's Transformative Impact as Assisted by Intradisciplinary Integration." In *Scholars Crossing Doctoral Dissertations and Projects*. PhD diss., John W. Rawlings School of Divinity, 2022.

Stringer, Ernest T., and Alfredo Ortiz Aragón. *Action Research*. 5th ed. Los Angeles: SAGE, 2020.

Syahdin, et al. "Stephen's Ministry Concept as a Transformative Deacon Prototype Model Based on Acts 6:5 in Pontianak City." *Technium Social Sciences Journal* 48 (2023) 320–30.

Tan, Siang-Yang. "Applying Theology in the Psychology Classroom: Reflections on Integration in the Trenches for 35 Years." *Journal of Psychology and Christianity* 42 (2023) 59–68.

———. "Christian Cognitive and Strength-Based Therapy." In *The Popular Encyclopedia of Christian Counseling: An Indispensable Tool for Helping People with Their Problems*. Edited by Tim Clinton and Ron Hawkins. Eugene, OR: Harvest House, 2011.

———. "Dealing with Spiritual Struggles in Psychotherapy: Empirical Evidence and Clinical Applications from a Christian Perspective." *Journal of Psychology and Christianity* 41 (2022) 311–16.

Taylor, Mark. *1 Corinthians*. The New American Commentary, vol. 28. Nashville: Broadman & Holman, 2014.

Bibliography

Thiselton, Anthony C. *Colossians: A Short Exegetical and Pastoral Commentary.* Eugene, OR: Cascade, 2020.

Thomas Aquinas. *Commentary on the Gospel of John, Chapters 6–12.* Translated by Fabian Larcher and James A. Weisheipl. Washington, DC: Catholic University of America Press, 2010.

Thompson, Curt. *Anatomy of the Soul: Surprising Connections Between Neuroscience and Spiritual Practices That Can Transform Your Life and Relationships.* Carol Stream, IL: Tyndale House, 2010.

Timoney, Martin Bernard. "Identifying the Core Components of Christian Humility." In *Scholars Crossing Doctoral Dissertations and Projects.* PhD diss., John W. Rawlings School of Divinity, 2020.

Tozer, A. W. *The Crucified Life.* In *The Essential Tozer Collection*, three-in-one ed. Compiled and edited by James L. Snyder. Minneapolis: Bethany House, 2013.

———. *The Knowledge of the Holy.* In *The Essential Tozer Collection*, three-in-one ed. Compiled and edited by James L. Snyder. Minneapolis: Bethany House, 2013.

Vanderstelt, Heather, et al. "Transformational Education: Exploring the Lasting Impact of Students' Clinical Pastoral Education Experiences." *Journal of Health Care Chaplaincy* 29 (2022) 89–104.

Van der Watt, Stéphan. "Mission-Minded Pastoral Theology and the Notion of God's Power: Maturity Through Vulnerability." *In die Skriflig* 57 (2023) 1–10.

Wells, Pamela C., and Kristen N. Dickens. "Creativity in Counselor Education: More than Case Studies." *International Journal for the Advancement of Counselling* 42 (2020) 191–99.

Wesley, John. *The Witness of the Spirit: A Sermon on Romans 8:16.* Bristol: William Pine, 1776. https://archive.org/details/bim_eighteenth-century_the-witness-of-the-spiri_wesley-john_1797/mode/2up.

White, Kristen M. "Conceptualizing Therapy as a Spiritual Discipline." *Journal of Psychology and Christianity* 39 (2020) 91–103.

Whitney, Donald S. *Spiritual Disciplines for Christian Life.* Revised and Updated. Colorado Springs, CO: NavPress, 2014.

Wilkins, Richard L. "Educating the Congregation on the Role of the Pastoral Counselor." In *Scholars Crossing Doctoral Dissertations and Projects.* PhD diss., John W. Rawlings School of Divinity, 2021.

Subject Index

attitude, 3, 8–9, 11, 37, 52, 71, 107, 137

behavior(s), ix, xiii, 2, 7–10, 12, 19, 24, 29, 35–37, 46, 48–51, 53–54, 62, 68, 73, 82, 91, 98, 102, 112, 117, 124, 127, 132–33, 157, 160
Bible, 2, 3, 5, 12–13, 17, 26, 29--30, 39, 42, 46, 49, 58–59, 72, 77, 85, 96, 107, 109, 111, 115–16, 118, 122, 129, 132, 159
biblical,
   application(s), 13, 22, 52, 65, 72, 115–16
   approach, 66, 78
   counseling, 28, 50, 158
   leadership, 1
   literacy, 35–36, 63, 65, 75, 79, 86, 102, 107–8, 110–11, 115–18, 122, 126, 131
   mindset, 65
   perspective, 4, 77, 91, 100–101, 109, 122
   principle(s), 2, 33, 35, 56
   thinking, x, 2–3, 14–15, 23, 50, 57–59, 61, 64–68, 71–73, 75, 90, 110–11, 113–14, 118–19, 126–27

truth(s), 2, 9
worldview, 1, 3, 35–37, 46, 59, 62, 65, 67, 77, 115, 126, 159

Christian,
   behavior, 10, 112
   character, 37, 159
   church, x, 2, 4, 34
   Cognitive Therapy (CCT), xiii, 48–49, 62, 132
   conduct, 9
   counseling, 22, 32, 38–39, 157–59, 161
   counselor. *See* counselor.
   education, xiii, 16–18, 29–30, 33–38, 61–62, 158, 160–61
   Integrative Therapeutic (CIT), xi, xiii, 2, 108
   Intrapersonal Formation (CIF), x–xi, xiii, 2–4, 10, 13–18, 24, 27–28, 30, 32, 34–36, 39–40, 43, 45, 50, 53, 56–59, 61–67, 69–70, 72–75, 77, 85, 100, 102–3, 107–14, 119, 122–24, 126–29
intrapersonal growth, 57
worldview, 17, 19, 22, 29, 54, 59, 61, 157

Subject Index

Christianity, ix, 9, 17–18, 29, 31, 34–35, 37–38, 47, 112, 118, 157–59, 161–62

Christlikeness, ix, x, 2–3, 8–9, 12–13, 16, 18, 29, 32–33, 36, 38, 40, 45, 47, 49, 52, 55, 59, 61, 64, 72, 79, 86, 99, 107, 109, 111–12, 117–18, 120

church, ix, x–xi, 1–2, 4–12, 15–16, 22–27, 29–30, 33–38, 47, 49, 55–56, 64–66, 69–70, 75–77, 79–83, 85, 89–98, 112, 114, 120, 121, 124, 128–29, 138, 158, 160–61

cognition, 20, 37, 56–57, 95, 121, 157

Cognitive Behavior Therapy (CBT), xiii, 48, 50–51, 133, 157, 160

conflict,
    cognitive, 75
    inner, 75, 83
    internal, xi, 27, 69, 83, 111, 114
    intrapersonal, 1, 4, 11–12, 14, 16, 20–23, 28, 32, 34, 39, 48, 52–55, 57–58, 61, 63–66, 68, 70–72, 75, 77–78, 81, 84, 107–8, 110, 113–17, 121–28, 130–31
    resolution, 22, 77, 111
    spiritual, ix, 38, 58,

counselor,
    Christian, 34, 49, 86
    education, 4, 19, 162
    pastoral, 15, 22, 28, 32–33, 48, 51–52, 54, 57, 60, 62–67, 69–72, 74–75, 78, 89, 109, 125, 162
    proactive pastoral, 2, 4, 27, 37–38, 64, 66, 69–70, 74, 100
    trainees, 19, 21, 34, 63, 71, 87, 159

discipleship, 13–14, 16–17, 27, 30–39, 51, 53, 56, 61, 69, 74, 79, 115–16, 127, 130, 157–58

emotion(s), 20, 25, 27, 65, 80, 87, 90–93, 95, 98–99, 101–2, 108, 110, 117, 119–20, 122, 132

emotional, 33–34, 54–55, 62, 64, 70–71, 83, 87, 102, 109, 124, 132–33

faith-based, 23, 28, 32, 38, 58, 63

God's Word, x, 2–5, 13–15, 17, 21–22, 24, 27, 29–30, 32, 35, 39–40, 43, 45–48, 50, 54–55, 57, 59, 61, 77, 93–95, 98–99, 110–11, 116, 118, 123, 128, 130

Holy Spirit, v, x–xi, 4, 6–7, 14–15, 18, 20–22, 24, 26, 30–32, 35, 38–39, 41–42, 45, 51–52, 57, 59–60, 73–74, 97, 116, 118, 123, 125–27, 130, 132, 135

identity, 9, 51–53, 61, 66, 71–73, 78, 157

inner dialogue(s), 19, 21, 51, 68, 95, 114, 121, 123, 160

Integrative Perspective (IP), xiii, 28, 32, 51, 61, 71

Integrative Therapy (IT), xiii, 51

interpersonal,
    chaos, 11
    communication, 18, 37, 63, 70, 75, 96, 114, 131
    conflict, 12
    conversation(s), 51
    movement, 71
    processes, 78

intrapersonal. *See* conflict.

mental, 2, 20–21, 28, 33, 50, 54, 60, 121, 160

Narrative Therapy (NT), xiii, 48, 53, 55, 133, 158–59

Subject Index

pastoral,
  care, 34, 159
  counseling, vii, xi-xiii, 3, 14, 16,
    19, 22–23, 28–29, 31–39, 48,
    50, 56, 58–60, 62, 64, 66, 75,
    123, 126–27, 158–59
  counselor, 15, 22, 28, 32–33, 48,
    51–52, 54, 57, 60, 62–67,
    69–72, 74, 77–78, 89, 109,
    125, 162
Proactive,
  Pastoral Counseling (PPC),
    xi-xii, 2, 4, 13, 23, 29, 53,
    56, 60–64, 72, 75–77, 85,
    108–10, 112, 114–15, 117,
    120, 126, 128–29, 132, 134
  pastoral counselor, 2, 4, 27, 37–
    38, 64, 66, 69–70, 74, 100

Rational Emotive Behavior Therapy
  (REBT), xiii, 48, 51, 54, 160
relationship,
  counselor-client, 32, 39, 64, 75,
    78, 109, 117, 125, 157
resolve, 21, 50, 53, 60, 91, 113,
    115–16, 121, 123, 127
resolution, 21–22, 60, 63, 68–70,
    77, 111

self,
  acceptance, 54, 132, 160
  aware(ness), 19, 27, 30, 49, 58,
    69, 86, 107–8, 110, 115,
    117–19, 131
  care, 34
  centered, ix, 2–4, 7, 15, 66
  centeredness, v, 66
  critical, 51
  criticism, 121
  defining, 53
  denial, 27
  derived, 8
  efficacy, 20
  esteem, 11, 54, 63, 66, 79–80, 83,
    114, 120, 133

examination, 41
hate, 83
healing, 127
help, 53, 81
identities, 34
identity, 53, 72, 157
judgment, 81
management, 121
managing, 51
perception, 69, 72
preservation, 1, 93, 97
preserving, 112
pursuits, 93
reflect(ion), 3, 18–19, 34, 53, 61,
    63, 77
reinforcement, 121
talk, 18–20, 51, 54–55, 68, 114,
    121, 160
thought(s), 50
thinking, 46, 119, 122–23
transcendence, 160
understanding, 7
worship, 13, 27
worth, 6, 66, 79
selfhood, 53
small group(s), 33, 51, 63–64, 66,
    69–70, 77–78, 89, 93–96,
    108, 110, 114, 116–17, 120,
    124
spiritual,
  applications, 29, 33, 35, 70, 77,
    89, 109, 115
  conflict, ix, 38, 57–58
  decline, 7, 94
  disciplines, 3, 13, 18, 20, 26–30,
    33, 35, 38–39, 52, 58–59,
    74–75, 79, 85–86, 99, 107,
    110–11, 116–18, 123, 126,
    132, 160, 162
  growth, 2, 13, 15, 25–31, 33,
    35–36, 39, 51, 56, 91, 93,
    115, 120, 129
  health, 3, 12, 120–21, 126
Stephen's Ministry (SM), 49, 51, 55,
    133, 161

theological, 39–40, 56, 69, 87, 100,
103
theoretical, 48–50, 57, 61, 65–66, 74
training (CIF),
    class, 99, 107
    course, 66–67, 76, 79, 85, 100,
    106, 108

program, 2–3, 16, 64–65, 77,
79–80, 85–86, 99, 103, 109,
112, 115–17, 124, 126–29

well-being, 13, 15, 20, 29–30, 32,
39, 54, 69, 87, 89, 102, 109,
113–14, 121–22, 124, 158

Scripture Index

Exodus
15:8-9	134
33:19	16

Deuteronomy
11:18-23	48, 138
11:19	46
18:15-19	39, 138
30:18-19	48, 13
30:18-23	48

Psalms
19:7-14	41, 139
62:1-2	95, 149
81:11	45, 140
118:8	72-73, 91, 149

Proverbs
2:1-5	140
2:1	48
3:5-6	77, 91, 147, 149
3:5-7	68
18:21	153
23:12	46, 140

Isaiah
40:31	95, 149
46:10	40, 140

Matthew
4:4	56, 140
5:1-2	40, 140
7:6	153
10:31	73, 149
11:28-30	39, 73, 111, 149, 153

Mark
12:31	62, 147

Luke
9:23-24	115, 154
9:23	42, 59, 78, 91, 141, 147, 150
9:35	40, 43, 141
10:19	98, 150
24:27	43, 141

John
1:3-4	141
1:3	42
1:4	42

John (cont.)

1:14	40, 47, 141
1:17	43, 141
3:8	15, 134
4:14	42, 141
4:22	42, 141
6:53–58	40, 141
6:63	4, 21, 40, 43, 57, 59, 134, 142
7:51	10, 134
8:12	42, 142
11:25–26	43, 142
14:6	43, 142
15:12	48, 142

Acts

2:46–47	112, 154
7:51	7, 135
9:6	45, 142
9:18	42
9:20	42
9:18–20	142
17:24	15, 135
17:28	41, 142, 154
20:22	94, 150

Romans

7:14–25	41, 143
8:1	41, 143
8:5	93, 150
8:6–8	143
8:6	44
10:9–10	16, 39, 143
10:17	94, 150
12:2	43, 46, 57, 78, 112, 117, 119, 143, 150, 154

1 Corinthians

1:12–13	29, 144
1:18	39, 144
2:2	135
2:11–14	21, 135
2:12–13	113, 154
2:13	125, 130
2:14	11, 25, 31
4:13b	x
6:11–12	44, 144
11:1	10, 135

2 Corinthians

2:12–15	155
3:4–6	11, 135
3:6	24
5:14–17	45, 144
5:17	73, 150
5:18–19	61
5:18–20	147
5:19	17, 61, 136
5:20	61, 112, 155
10:4–5	95, 150
10:5	14, 39–40, 46, 73, 136, 144
12:9	41, 145

Galatians

5:16–18	92, 151
5:16	45, 145

Ephesians

4:17–18	24, 136
4:22–23	24
4:22–24	77, 136, 145, 151, 155
4:23	43, 45, 63, 112
4:32	62, 148
6:10–17	94, 151

Philippians

2:1–5	11, 64, 136
2:8–11	145
2:10	44
2:12–13	14

Scripture Index

4:7	42, 145
4:8	99, 152

Colossians

3:1–2	119, 146, 155
3:2	47
3:16	48

1 Thessalonians

2:4	10, 137
5:19	11, 137

1 Timothy

2:3–4	146, 156
2:4	44, 72, 111
4:1–2	9, 96, 137, 152
4:6–7	146
4:6	45–46
4:7	40, 44, 115, 156

2 Timothy

3:14–15	47
3:14–17	77, 152
3:16–17	41, 146

Hebrews

1:2–4	146
1:2	43
1:3	17, 41–42, 47
3:1–4	137
4:12	40
11:1	93, 152
11:2	44
12:1–3	130

James

1:4	115, 156
1:19–21	153
1:19	98
1:21	43, 73, 147
1:22	61

1 Peter

1:3–6	79
1:6–7	153
5:7	91

1 John

2:15	111, 156
3:21	77, 153

Revelation

3:1–4	4, 138

www.ingramcontent.com/pod-product-compliance
Lightning Source LLC
Chambersburg PA
CBHW050809160426
43192CB00010B/1691